THE LIFE
I NEVER KNEW
I WANTED

THE LIFE
I NEVER KNEW
I WANTED

A Memoir About Camping, Family, and What Happens When We Get Off the Beaten Path

SARAH STYF

SHIFTING PERSPECTIVE PRESS

"Not all who wander are lost." – J.R.R. Tolkien

To Jeff, Lydia, and Ethan. Thank you for being a constant part of my camping journey. The world is a better place because you are wandering it with me.

Contents

Prologue

WE PULLED INTO OUR site in McKinney Falls State Park right before sunset. The June heat was already unseasonably oppressive, even after the sun went down. Our single air-conditioner struggled to lower the inside temperature. The travel trailer's aluminum sides were ineffectively insulated against the dark heat that still hung in the 90s, with little chance that the thermometer would drop to the 80s by morning.

Our nearly-seven-year-old grabbed the wheel chocks and helped me put them into place before helping my husband Jeff remove the hitch and lower the front jack. I watched Ethan proudly walk around the camper with a drill in hand, taking sole responsibility for putting down the stabs that would keep our camper steady while we remained parked for the weekend.

We woke up to the sun rising over the cypress, oaks, and junipers of Texas Hill Country, right outside of Austin. The day ahead involved escaping the heat at a local waterpark before taking our daughter and bat-loving little boy into downtown Austin to watch the Mexican free-tailed bats fly out from underneath the Congress Avenue bridge at sunset. That evening, we climbed onto the tour boat on the shores of Lady Bird Lake and sailed around the perimeter. The tour guide highlighted the sights around the lake surrounded by the expansive state capital.

As we floated underneath the Congress Avenue Bridge, each of us looked up into the ironworks to see hundreds of thousands of tiny bodies curled up into nests under the busy city bridge. They were little creatures completely unaware of the hundreds of observers lining both sides of the bridge above them or resting in boats below on the lake, waiting for the approach of dusk. Suddenly one took off, then a dozen, then a swarm of 750,000 hungry, pregnant bats flew off into the night to rid local farms of flying insects.

When we landed back on the shore, the lights of the city guided us back to our car so we could return to the quiet of the campground. It was dark, and with two tired kids, we decided to take a shortcut back to our parked truck. We walked them through the Hyatt Hotel, right on the shores of the lake. They looked around in awe, full of wonder that people actually slept there while on vacation. When Jeff stopped with our son in the bathroom on our way out, Ethan chattered away, asking what people do in the hotel and why they would want to stay there when they could just go camping.

"Well, there are some people who just don't like camping," Jeff told him.

Our son, still standing in front of the hotel bathroom urinal, exclaimed, "That's just preposterous!"

One thing became clear in that moment. Ethan couldn't understand a world in which people would choose to be surrounded by air-conditioned restaurants, heated pools, access to exercise equipment, a clean bed, and a spacious bathroom.

All he knew was a life where his parents towed our hotel room behind us and his first duty upon arrival was finding the bathroom and playground. He didn't spend his nights in a new location being told to quietly walk down hallways or avoid stomping on the floor and disturbing the people below. Instead, he and his big sister spent their evenings riding bikes and sitting in front of a campfire. It wasn't that he couldn't be persuaded to appreciate hotel stays; he just didn't understand why he should have to.

I laughed when Jeff relayed the story to me later, complete with Ethan's mid-pee exclamation. This was the life we had created for our family, and clearly my children had no regrets.

The next morning, we woke up and hiked across the rocky plain to McKinney Falls. Lydia and Ethan jumped from rock to rock and hopped over puddles and streams of clear water leading to the Lower Falls, where we found park visitors jumping into the cool water below. We waded in the water streaming toward the cliff's edge, then returned to the camper so we could check out before the heat became more than we could handle. Four hours later, we would be settled back into our air-conditioned Houston home.

It was just as our little boy stated. Anything else would be preposterous.

Chapter 1
My Fiancé Convinces Me to Go Camping

Here is an important truth: I did not grow up a camping girl. I loved the outdoors and I loved nature, but for the first twenty-two years of my life I equated camping with dirt and mosquitoes, peeing in suffocatingly foul outhouses, and cooking hot dogs and tin foil meals over a hard-to-build fire. It was all an equation for a total lack of necessary comforts and collapsing tents.

Here is a second important truth: Finding the right partner in life means finding someone who will challenge you to grow, try new things, and give you nudges at the right time in the right place.

I'm not sure what convinced my husband Jeff that I could convert from a girl-who-preferred-indoor-lodging to a girl-who-eagerly-sought-out-places-to-pitch-a-tent. When we met the summer before heading off to college, camping adventures were the last thing on my mind. Any time he brought up his family memories of years camping around Michigan and Indiana, all I could think about was the amount of work it must take for a family of six to camp on a vacation when one could just carry suitcases into a friend or family member's house—or, if absolutely necessary, a clean hotel room.

Despite getting at least one tour of the small camper that sat unused in his parent's side yard, I believed Jeff wanted to take me out into the wilderness with a tent and simple equipment. My boyfriend, however, wasn't trying to convince me to go off the grid or join him and the guys on a Canadian fishing trip. He just wanted me to consider sleeping in a tent within driving distance of a grocery store.

We started dating on a whim, two teenagers just finishing high school and getting ready for the next big step in life. Mutual friends introduced us to each other and he invited me to watch Fourth of July fireworks with him at the beach. Then he asked me to go to a movie. And then we were spending every spare moment with each other.

I had no intention of marrying him. I just wanted a fling. Our differences extended beyond his love of camping and roughing it and my personal desires for a hotel room. I was a studious bookworm; he was a computer geek who loved learning but hated going to school. I was a perfectionist afraid to upset the balance of the universe; he didn't appear to care what anyone thought of him. I was a rule follower; he was a prankster with a long list of infractions. I was going to college in Nebraska; he remained in Michigan to continue his schooling.

But over time we discovered we had more in common than we didn't. And the six hundred miles apart actually helped us grow individually and as a couple. When he encouraged me to apply for a study abroad program in England during my junior year, the three-and-a-half months away helped us both realize just how much we eventually wanted to merge our life paths moving forward.

He just had to convince me to do that life together inside of a tent first.

His opportunity arose the summer before we got married. Two of my college friends were tying the knot in Cheyenne, Wyoming, and I saw this as the perfect chance for us to take a cross-country trip to attend the wedding and also visit Jeff's sister in Denver, Colorado. At twenty-two, these travel plans were an assertion of young adult independence. For four years I had spent most of my time living six hundred miles from home and away from a boyfriend who not everyone in my family thought I should marry. In seven months, Jeff and I would be entering married bliss and a big part of me wanted to prove I could be an independent woman instead of a dutiful eldest daughter.

We *needed* to do this. For the duration of our relationship, the only times we regularly saw each other were during school breaks when we were both home at our parents' houses—still right around the corner from each other in our small, southwest Michigan hometown. This trip felt like it held more potential for bonding and testing than any premarital counseling session. It was also my chance to convince Jeff that my reasonable dreams of living in Colorado needed to become a reality as soon as possible.

My immediate family lived in central Wyoming during a large part of my adolescence. It was a period that slowly broke some—but not all—of my Detroit-bred city girl ways. During those years, we made several trips to visit my mom's aunts and uncles in the Denver area, taking us away from our large Wyoming town and into a big city surrounded by the Rockies. And to put it simply, I loved it. I loved the dry climate and nearly daily sunshine. I loved the wide-open spaces with the snow-capped mountains rising in the distance. I loved rocky hiking trails and rushing mountain rivers.

When our family moved back to Michigan right before my junior year of high school, I dreamed of returning out west and moving to Denver, a plan that would give me the best of both worlds: city and close proximity to mountains. I would have access to culture and shopping and everything I needed, with an escape to nature whenever the desire hit.

Part of me was excited to show my fiancé a place I wanted us to move to as soon as we had the chance, praying he would be as enamored as I was. But most of me dreaded the very idea of camping and being out in nature without easy access to modern conveniences. I was convinced this was going to be several times more difficult than the three years I had traveled up into the mountains for summer youth camp, where we had access to full bathrooms, bunk beds, and regularly cooked meals we just had to show up for. I had no idea what to expect. I didn't want to look like a wimp and disappoint my future husband, and I feared embarrassing myself in front of his big sister and all of her friends.

We were young and excited for a road trip away from parents and summer responsibilities. We drove all day and through the night in my Mercury Topaz, switching off sleeping and driving every two hours or so. We traveled across the desolate western Nebraska land-scape, the dark stretch of I-80 in front of us for hundreds of miles. Hungry and sleep-deprived, we neared the equally barren eastern border of Colorado as the sun rose.

Our safe arrival in Denver was quickly followed by helping my future sister-in-law pack up her car with all of the equipment we would need for a few days of camping. I quickly realized I knew noth-ing about outdoor living as I watched Kristen pull out of her closet carefully packed and organized totes to carry out to our vehicles. I had no idea there were so many accessories required for staying in tents, nor did I understand just how seriously people could take the entire experience.

In less than two hours, we had packed two vehicles full of equip-ment and were ready to go. Jeff drove my little black car up through increasing altitudes and switchbacks. The whole vehicle groaned as he shifted the manual transmission multiple times to find just the right gear to get us up the mountain. Our church-based premarital counseling had told us we scored high on communication, but that test had included nothing about real-life experience. We both be-gan to wonder—how much stress could two sleep-deprived twen-ty-two-year-olds endure before one of them exploded at the other?

When we finally arrived at the YMCA of the Rockies in Winter Park, I got a crash course in setting up camp—from Colorado residents for whom camping was a way of life. Everybody knew what they needed to do and where they should put their equipment and how to put everything together. It was like watching ballet, and I had never been given the chance to learn the steps. No one complained, no one questioned, and no one was without a job.

Once the expansive campsite and tent city were set up, I took time to investigate our accommodations. I realized we were surround-ed by a perfect balance of nature and modern amenities. We could still have bacon and eggs and pancakes cooked on stoves for break-fast. And there were available bathrooms within a decent walking distance from our campsite. That meant I could still keep myself semi-presentable for my fiancé—something I was far more concerned about than I should have been in that season of my life.

As the sun started to set over the treetops, someone found wood to build a campfire. Multiple people pitched in to prepare dinner. For the first time, I experienced the great fellowship and joy of a camping circle.

The sunset eventually turned to night. We arrived in Colorado in late May, the last remnants of winter snow still sitting on top of most mountain peaks. Nights in the Rocky Mountains are cold, regardless of the time of year. Although I'd made sure we had enough warm gear to keep us from freezing, the chill still seeped into my bones. Dressed in multiple layers, all the way down to the socks that covered my toes, I snuggled into Jeff's eager arms, more for additional warmth than affection.

The next morning, Jeff and I awoke groggy. Both of us were still recovering from driving across the country and then spending the next night drinking. But we convinced ourselves we could keep up with his sister Kristen and her roommate Sandy; if they could do it, so could we. How quickly we were proven to be the mountain newbies we were.

Looking back over 20 years later, it's easy to see how we were able to so naively believe we could handle whatever the mountains had to throw at us. While we have never been in peak physical condition, Jeff and I both love hiking. We enjoy exploring new terrains, wandering through woods and over rocky streams, and seeing how many steps and stairs we can get on our fitness trackers. Our love for long walks and hiking explorations started on our very first date when we spent several hours walking up and down the Lake Michigan shoreline following the Fourth of July fireworks. And this wouldn't be the only hike we took during our Colorado trip. A couple of days later, we would find ourselves hiking and touring our way through the Garden of the Gods.

But this was a morning when we were both tired and dehydrated, and Jeff had never been in the mountains before. In the course of two days, we had climbed nearly two miles in elevation, not slept, completely changed from a humid Midwestern climate to the dry high-desert, and had probably consumed half the amount of water we were supposed to drink to stay healthy.

Not long into the hike, I realized Jeff had slowed down and his face turned a sickly gray. After he ran into the bushes to vomit up his entire breakfast, the rest of us looked at each other and stupidly realized the reason for his sluggish behavior: altitude sickness.

I force-fed him gulps of water while he sat down to recover, and eventually we started to slowly work our way back to the tent. Back at the campsite, he collapsed into his sleeping bag and didn't say another word for hours.

I have never dealt with illness well, especially when vomit is involved, and Jeff didn't just feel miserable. He looked like he had been run over by a moose. I had no idea how to help him. There I was, seven months before I would promise love and faithfulness to my fiancé for the rest of my life, and I felt like I was already failing the sickness part of my future marriage vows.

But I did what I could. I made sure he stayed hydrated, regularly checked on him while he slept, and made sure all of his needs were met. When he agreed to stop for pizza at a roadside parlor on our way down the mountain, I began to realize we had weathered the storm together.

And the funniest part of the whole trip? I really enjoyed the camping part of our adventure. I laughed while watching Jeff and one of Kristen's friends knock down a dead tree stump that we used to feed our fire all weekend long. I enjoyed the hiking—until Jeff got sick—and appreciated the distraction-free opportunity to bond with my future sister-in-law. I happily played card games under a screen tent, reaching for my wine cooler to take another sip before laying down the next card.

The following week, before we headed up to Wyoming for the wedding that had been the original excuse for our trip, we spent an afternoon at Target filling out our wedding registry, complete with enough camping equipment to get us started on our own camping adventures. Several months later, when we got the Coleman camp stove and sleeping bags we had asked for, we knew we were on our way to a marriage full of outdoor vacations.

Camping and travel adventures became central to our story. It's become an integral part of the ups and downs of our marriage. It has woven itself into our dreams, both those fulfilled and those left unrealized. It's played an important role through swerves in our path, both the good and bad. It's been responsible for creating friendships and family bonds. It's taken us from a dome tent to a travel trailer with a map of the United States we are slowly filling in, one new location at a time.

But I had so much to learn along the way.

Chapter 2
I Wasn't Raised a Camping Girl

I WAS A PRINCESS. No, I was an explorer. Nope, I was just trying to escape the noise and chaos coming from my two younger sisters.

I unzipped the front screen and crawled out into a field of yellow dandelions, violets, and four-leaf clovers. My flying horse was safely harnessed to the metal rungs of my playset. Wooden boards hedged the expanse of smooth, fine grains in my sandbox. The three-foot high chain link fence surrounding our corner lot was invisible to me. So was the alley immediately behind our brick garage and the neat rows of 1930s bungalows that made up our neighborhood in the middle of Detroit's concrete jungle.

Whether I was by myself or playing with my little sisters and neighborhood friends, the backyard was my tiny escape, a place where my imagination could run wild. And that playtime was enhanced by every installation we added to that small patch of green.

I got my first tent when I was about six or seven. It was small, emerald, and triangular, the type that would fit a single adult, a sleeping bag, and a small duffle. To this day, I have no idea what prompted my maternal grandparents to buy a tent for my two younger sisters and me. My parents weren't campers. And while they both grew up in country settings, the first nine years of my life involved my family going out into nature only during the occasional visits to my grandparents' farm near Ionia, Michigan.

I don't think my grandparents ever believed a single gift would turn into a family hobby of outdoor exploration, but we loved that tent all the same. We set it up in our backyard and escaped from the reality of our urban neighborhood into different worlds of our own making. Our faces baked in the tent as summer temperatures climbed, and we never could quite escape the distinctive nylon smell as we sat inside. But still, we invited neighborhood friends over to climb in and out of the single flap door, unzipping the window on the opposite end to allow anyone else to look at and talk to those inside.

Months into our new adventures, one night we left the tent outside and woke up the next morning to discover our tent, stakes and all, had disappeared out of the backyard. Someone had climbed the chain link fence into our backyard and decided they needed it more than us. At the time, we were devastated. I remember crying when discovering the tent's absence. But my sisters and I quickly returned to our swing set and sandbox over the following days and moved on to new adventures.

I grew up a city girl in nearly every sense. As a preschooler, I learned how to carefully cross our busy street so I could play with those friends who lived only a couple of houses away. Once I was in elementary school, my mom would occasionally let me walk with other neighborhood kids to the playground a couple of streets away, but it was little more than swings and a merry-go-round on a concrete pad. My parochial elementary school in the middle of the city didn't have a playground or green space. When it was nice enough for us to play outside, we ran around on concrete and blacktop parking lots just outside the building and within the surrounding tall chain link fences.

But my mom grew a productive garden nearly every summer. We went to the zoo in Royal Oak and went on school field trips to Belle Isle in the middle of the Detroit River. Every couple of years, my dad would plan a trip to visit his maternal and paternal grandmothers and the Iowa farms of his aunts and uncles. And whenever time would allow, my mom made sure we took trips out to visit our grandparents on the farm where she grew up.

There was always a kind of dissonance between our urban lives and these trips to the country, one filled with more questions than answers. Were the trees between the house and the field for climbing, or were we supposed to stay out of them? Were we allowed to play with the barn cats, or should we leave them alone? What were we supposed to do with our grandparents' large German shepherd? When we walked out into the woods just across from their house, how far were we allowed to explore before we had wandered too far from our parents?

We didn't have things like family pets or trees or large, open fields at home. And when outdoor mishaps happened, I often wasn't prepared for them. I remember one particular hike through the woods when I fell off a log and stepped into the creek running through the forest. It was fall. The water was frigid. I didn't know how to handle both my wet shoes and the seeping cold that settled into my body. I was mostly eager to return to the house where I could put on dry clothes and sit in a temperature-controlled environment.

Nature was always something to admire from a distance, not usually to experience up close and personal. We didn't avoid the outdoors; we just usually avoided close interaction with the *wild* outdoors, staying on established paths and at a close distance from non-domestic animals. As a result, I did not grow up in a family who would consider camping for any reason. It was a fact that makes the two memorable exceptions to that rule all the more significant.

Chapter 3
A Disastrous Camping Trip

THE FIRST EXCEPTION TO our family's no-camping practice happened when I was in middle school. My maternal grandparents purchased a camper just before my grandmother retired. For their 40th wedding anniversary, my grandparents made it clear they didn't want a big celebration and instead wanted a family reunion with their four children and their families. Plans were made, and each family reserved a site at Ludington State Park in Michigan.

At the time my family was living in Wyoming, where my dad served as both principal and teacher for our church's elementary school. So for our family's very first camping trip, we drove halfway across the country, back to Midwestern humidity, to use borrowed camping equipment for this singular family outing. I have hazy memories of walking along the wooded shores of Lake Michigan with my three-month-older cousin and yelling across a bay at boys who were probably too old for us and not nearly as cute up close as we both assumed they were from a distance.

In the mornings we ate breakfast prepared by my uncles in their self-constructed outdoor kitchen. My perfectly groomed grandmother—a woman who returned to college to complete her degree after all of her children were out of the house, proudly worked at the Chamber of Commerce for her small Michigan town, and had convinced my country boy grandfather to travel to Western Europe and then Eastern Europe immediately following the fall of the Berlin Wall—reveled in having her four children and all of her grandchildren with her in the great outdoors. She traded her formal dining room for picnic tables set end to end and prepared meals to the best of her ability to ensure none of us missed the comforts of their 1800s farmhouse.

Even with my aversion to dirt, my fear of mosquitoes, my desire for a bed that wasn't on the ground, and my adolescent insistence on carrying my pink Caboodle to the bathrooms every morning so I could be perfectly made up, I fell in love with one of the prettiest state parks I have ever visited in the northern Midwest. But I was still certain camping was something for people who didn't mind bugs and being dirty. Nature was great and it wasn't *that* scary. In fact, the couple of years we had already spent in Wyoming had begun to open those doors for me even before my grandparents forced us into our first outdoor trip.[1] But if my parents thought that they were going to get me to go camping in a tent again, they had another think coming.[2]

Despite my adolescent consternation, the trip to Ludington awakened in my parents the many possibilities of family camping that the rest of us didn't realize existed. A couple of years later, Mom and Dad decided we were going to camp our way through the Black Hills as we visited family and friends along the northern half of the United States. My mom, a lifelong Laura Ingalls Wilder fan, dreamed of visiting the Ingalls Wilder home in De Smet, South Dakota, and my parents saw this as an opportunity to visit sites such as Mount Rushmore, the Black Hills, and Devil's Tower.

---

1. I went on one tent-camping trip with my Girl Scout troop in seventh grade. And despite the competence of my troop leaders, it also failed to convince me of the value of camping.

2. Funny enough, I didn't even remember my family had returned to Michigan the following summer for another family camping trip with two of my mom's three brothers and their families. Apparently, it didn't make nearly the impression the first family trip made. As I was writing and researching for this book, my mom pulled out pictures from two separate summers as proof.

But quality camping equipment doesn't run cheap. My parents wanted to be sure our family could make the camping thing stick before they risked spending money on new traveling supplies with their single-income church worker's budget. They borrowed one canvas tent from church friends, and my uncle offered to send them his small dome tent, large enough for two adolescent girls. We packed a cooler for food along the way, suitcases for our clothes, a couple of flashlights, and little else.

I was 15 by the time of this experiment. And while it had been proven to me that I could survive sleeping outdoors, I really had no desire to go camping with my family in such cramped quarters. It was hard enough being a teenage girl forced to visit national monuments and historic sites that I wasn't one-hundred percent convinced were cool. After all, why couldn't we return to visit my parents' friends in southern California like we did when I was nine, or make the long journey to see places like Washington, D.C.?

While I looked forward to seeing one of my best friends who at the time lived in South Dakota, and I was secretly interested in the historical sites behind the *Little House* books, this was not the vacation of my teenage dreams. And in a tent? Honestly, I just wanted a bug-free, air-conditioned hotel room and the rare treat of a heated pool. But the family budget limited our options, and my parents' hearts had heard the sudden call to adventure. So we went.

We were novice campers with borrowed equipment we had never used before heading into the Black Hills, a region notorious for sudden (and sometimes violent) thunderstorms. The four of us girls ranged in age from four to 15, and my 40-year-old parents had never camped on their own before. In short, it was a recipe for disaster.

On the first night of our trip, we stopped at Devil's Tower and settled into the campground. The weather was near perfect, dry and cool. The campground was showing *Close Encounters of the Third Kind*, Steven Spielberg's 1977 classic that he filmed on top of the national monument. Since our family didn't have any real interest in the sci-fi movie, we spent time at our campsite. But we didn't have much in the way of campsite entertainment, my desire to read fighting against the waning light and lack of lanterns. Since my younger sisters typically had much earlier bedtimes, we were all ready for bed by the time the sun went down.

Anticipation hung in the air. The natural rock tower rising amidst the surrounding pines had captured our imaginations. All of us excitedly waited for sunrise, eager to do some exploring and possibly climb as many rocks as the park rangers would allow. I dreamed of climbing the rock face, ignoring the training and equipment required. Maybe camping in a national park wasn't such a bad idea after all.

Lisa and I, the two older sisters, got to sleep in the little green dome tent, giving us some much-needed teen separation from the rest of the family. My parents and four-year-old Johanna and nine-year-old Rachel got the borrowed canvas tent. Rachel claims she told Mom and Dad she didn't trust the tent; it didn't seem it would hold up against the slight breeze that was building as the sun went down. But that didn't matter. These were the sleeping accommodations we had. There was no turning back now. And so everyone settled in for sleep.

In the years since that fateful night, I've learned to appreciate the awesome experience of a thunderstorm in a tent. Yes, there is some discomfort in being exposed to the elements and praying your rainfly will hold, that the lines won't go flapping in the wind, that nothing will crash on the thin nylon walls and metal tent poles which are the only thing standing between you and the torrential rain. But there is also something truly awe-inspiring and weirdly romantic about the natural drama, especially when cozying up to a lover. With a good tent, you might experience a mist that dampens some surfaces, a small price to pay for a front-seat view to the full-fledged power of nature.

But teenaged Sarah still had to learn this lesson...

Lisa and I quickly fell asleep, all cozy in our sleeping bags. An earth-shattering "Crack!" awakened us from our slumber, the blinding flashes of lightning causing us both to sit up. We were initially frightened by the blowing wind, torrential rain, and ear-splitting thunder accompanying the bursts of lightning through the dark night. Still, our rainfly kept us mostly dry. So we looked at each other and settled back into our sleeping bags, agreeing to wait out the storm.

Then we heard it, the screams and shouting from the next tent over as my parents rushed Rachel and Johanna into our minivan. Doors were thrust open and slammed shut while my parents yelled at each other to get the necessary supplies out of the rain and into the van.

Lisa's and my nervous giggles grew into peals of laughter as we realized the old canvas tent had collapsed on the rest of our family and they would be spending the night in the minivan. With no desire to go out into the pouring rain, we stayed put. Eventually, Lisa and I fell back asleep, still comfortable after the storm passed.

We awoke the next morning to a beautiful Wyoming sunrise and stories of woe from nine-year-old Rachel who accused us of laughing at her pain and the lack of fairness that our tent didn't collapse. Later that day, Dad, Lisa, and I got to use our dry shoes to climb on the fallen rocks surrounding the base of Devil's Tower. But Rachel grumpily parked her body on the ground below us, her tennis shoes far too soaked to allow for safe climbing.

From that point on, my sisters and I were done. My parents told us that it would be fine, that it couldn't rain like that every night. In response, we each told them we had no interest in continuing the camping adventure. It was time to admit we were motel people and we just needed to find a place with four solid walls and a roof for the remainder of our vacation.

Despite our protestations and insistence that they were outvoted four to two, we finished out the trip by camping along the way, with a couple of stops indoors to visit friends and family.[3] The entire family

---

3. By the time we got to Nebraska, where my dad had planned a long bike ride, our paternal grandparents picked up us kids to take us back to Kansas with them and my parents continued camping. It was going to be a hard sell to get us back into a tent for the trip home.

was done with camping by the time we returned home, all of us swearing off sleeping in a tent ever again.

It's because of this early tent trauma that, seven years later, my charming fiancé and I were both surprised when he convinced me to go camping with his sister. I think more than anything, I wanted to prove to Jeff I could and would try new things in our life together. But if not for him, my camping story would have ended after that Black Hills trip.

I'm glad he saw something in me that I didn't.

Chapter 4
Finding the Right Tent

In over twenty years of marriage, I have determined the two best activities for strengthening a relationship are camping and home improvement. Both activities will either bring a couple together or tear them apart by revealing every single weakness in the relationship. They will demonstrate what your partner is made of and destroy every façade you put up to try to win over your significant other.

When my baby sister Johanna got married, one of the items she and my new brother-in-law wanted most was a tent. Surprisingly, even after that disastrous family camping trip through the Black Hills, three of the four of us still eventually fell in love with camping, thanks to the encouragement of our outdoor-loving husbands.

Jeff and I put ourselves on tent-hunting/purchasing duty, and it quickly reminded me of our own early plans for married camping adventures. When we spent that afternoon at a Colorado Target working on our guest registry, I was still excited from our camping weekend and Jeff was quick to capitalize on it. We registered for nearly every item we thought we would need for camping someday—or at least everything Target carried at the time. Then we watched our gift registry with bated breath. We were only twenty-two and had very few of our own household items with which to start adult life together. But as much as we *needed* bedding, towels, and all manner of kitchen equipment, we *wanted* new camping gear.

Jeff's aunt and uncle hosted a couple's wedding shower at the tail end of my college Thanksgiving break, right before I would head back to Denver to finish my student teaching. We excitedly opened our

Coleman grill/stove combination, convinced it was all we needed to cook on the road. We received two bulky twenty-degree, fleece-lined sleeping bags that we could zip together for a single king-sized bed. They were perfect, we had decided, for newlywed love-making and cuddling on cold nights like the ones we had experienced while camping in Colorado. We also got a propane-powered lantern with extra mantles, which left us ready for nights cooking in the dark and sitting at a picnic table when we weren't gathered around a fire.

But our dream tent still sat on our registry, unpurchased.

As we got closer to spring and the opportunity to go camping together for the first time as a married couple, we finally made a withdrawal from our wedding gift money and purchased the Eddie Bauer tent from our registry. It would sleep six, which gave us plenty of room for a queen-sized air mattress, our sleeping bags, and duffle bags full of clothing and toiletries.

We thought that first tent purchase would last us quite a while, but Jeff and I have always been suckers for an end-of-season sale. A couple of years after we bought our first tent, we saw a clearance sticker on the Eddie Bauer tent of our dreams. It could sleep up to ten people. It had two thin nylon curtains we could hang to split the tent into three "rooms." It had pockets and places to hang storage for our keys, sunglasses, and wallets. And it had the perfect amount of room for us, our new dog, and someday a pack-and-play for at least one little human. From the first time we staked it in the ground, we called it the "Tent-Mahal," mostly because it was so large and grandiose in comparison to what we had before that we felt it needed a grandiose name.

Yes, it was probably more than we near-newlyweds needed, but we didn't care. It gave us—and our dreams—room to grow.

And when Johanna said she needed a new tent, we hoped to pass those dreams along to my baby sister and her soon-to-be husband.

Jeff had always been happy with a tent and a sleeping bag. But he's also a technophile constantly on the hunt for new gadgets, and camping was no exception. A battery-powered ceiling light/fan that attached to the top of our tent? We needed it immediately. Mini-propane powered heater? That would keep his wife warm and extend the season. New gadgets to keep insects at bay? We had to add them to the list.

I am a money-saving miser who wasn't ready to give up *all* of the comforts of home. I wanted a better air mattress so we didn't have to sleep on the ground. I agreed to the camp kitchen with a foot pump for "running" water because I wanted an easier way to do dishes. And the cast iron cooking set took some getting used to, but those pans sure made cooking food on a propane-powered stove easier once I figured out how to use them.

But we quickly learned accessories are only part of the outdoor living equation.

Our first independent camping trip as a couple didn't really count. For the first six months of marriage, we lived in a small town in southwest Michigan, waiting for me to find a full-time teaching job that would most likely take us out of the state. Once the snow melted, western Michigan provided plenty of viable locations for a test run with our newly-purchased dome tent and some of our equipment. We drove half an hour to Warren Dunes State Park and paid for a spot in the rustic campground. For me, it was roughing it: no electricity, no bathrooms with indoor plumbing, and an open field full of other campers and Boy Scout troops. But it was our dry run. We just wanted to have a single night to set up our tent and see how all of our new camping equipment would work for us.

Just a year before, my sister-in-law and her friends had made setting up a tent look so simple. Put together the poles, find the right holes, throw the rainfly on top of that, and voila, done.

If only it was that easy.

Even my experienced camping husband had to work through the instructions, figuring out which tent poles went on which sides of our tent and which poles went with the rainfly. And I, meanwhile, was completely lost.

I looked at the tent on the ground. I looked at the poles. And then I tried to figure out how in the world the manufacturers managed to get the tent to stretch from point A to point B without breaking a pole or ripping out the stitching along the outside edges. Tent manual in hand, my normally calm, laid-back husband stood next to me and grew increasingly agitated.

"Why aren't you listening to my instructions?" he hissed through the dark.

"Why aren't you *reading* the instructions?" I shot back.

Newlywed bliss disappeared as we attempted to work together without fighting in front of other campers near us. Instead, we communicated through frustrated grunts and occasional outbursts thrown in between long gaps of silence. What were we doing wrong?

The next couple of months presented other opportunities for us to work on setting up camp together. Our tent-building process slowly improved, and we could eventually construct it without the inevitable verbal crossfire. But it still took several more months before we could break down camp without elevated tension. I had to learn to practice patience with my knees in the dirt, folding up the tarp and wiping off the bottom of the tent as I attempted to roll it as tightly as possible, only to realize I had forgotten the tent poles, again. I repeatedly had to start all over to fit an even bulkier tent roll into the impossibly small bag the tent designers had provided for storage.

It took at least half a dozen trips before we both became comfortable with the process. It would be a couple of years before we were a well-oiled machine, as both a couple and a camping duo.

Of course, there were hiccups. The first time we put up the Tent-Mahal, we were camping with one of Jeff's work friends and his wife. By the time we arrived at the northern Indiana campground, it was nearing dusk. They had already started the process of setting up their pop-up camper, and we were left to figure out our new, bigger, much more complicated tent in the disappearing daylight. Frustrated, tired, hungry, and determined to get the tent set up before we started dinner, I bent one of the tent poles when I tried to put it in the wrong loop. It was not the way I wanted my birthday celebration weekend in Amish country to start, but by the time we were headed home, my frustrating pole incident was just one more story we could tell our future children. And Jeff was able to call the company and eventually get the pole replaced.

In the twelve years between our and Johanna's wedding, a lot had changed in tent camping technology. Now older and wiser, we couldn't get over the fact that every tent we found at major chain stores was an "easy-up" tent. Learning how to pitch a tent in the early years of our marriage had challenged our communication skills and forced us to deal with minor adversity long before we faced real problems. How could my sister and new brother-in-law truly grow as a couple if they weren't fighting over which poles went where?

But when the excited couple opened up the tent at Johanna's bridal shower and they immediately decided to put it up, I breathed a sigh of justified relief. Watching them struggle with even a simplified tent construction reminded me there were plenty of other camping challenges facing the newlyweds. Jeff and I didn't need to wish a ruined tent on them as well.

As we branched out and spent more time on the road, we learned the essentials of teamwork that prepared us for many of the marriage challenges that faced us down the road: patience, communication, presence, and natural existence without any effort. I hoped the same would be true for my newlywed sister as well.

Chapter 5
A Road Trip to Nebraska

DURING THAT FIRST YEAR of marriage, our camping trips were close to home and relatively close to civilization. We had little money and even less time off work. All of that changed as my grandparents' 50th wedding anniversary approached.

A year and a half after our wedding, we were now living in Indiana and in the process of buying our first house. My grandparents decided they wanted a family reunion with their seven children, their spouses, and 23 grandchildren to celebrate 50 years of marriage. My parents and aunts and uncles looked into various church camps and other places around the country that could offer fun local experiences and enough lodging for nearly 40 people ranging in age from early elementary school to early 70s. Even though no one in my extended family lived in the state and it was nowhere close to where anyone lived, the adults in charge of reunion planning selected Fort Robinson, a state park located in the middle of nowhere in northwest Nebraska.[1]

Jeff was less than thrilled when I proposed the trip to him. After three and a half years of him traveling from Michigan to Nebraska during our dating years, he thought he was done with trips to the Cornhusker State. I knew there was no way he'd choose the trip of

---

1. It wasn't until years later I discovered, while reading my grandmother's memoir, that Fort Robinson had been a family favorite for my grandparents and their young family when they lived in Nebraska. While I still might question the wisdom of the location, the choice suddenly made a lot more sense.

his own volition. So in my best conflict-avoidance mode, I pretended like it was a done deal for our summer vacation.

After listening to months of plans being bounced around, Jeff finally spoke up. "You want me to drive to Nebraska for a family reunion? And not just Nebraska, but western Nebraska? That's a *long* drive to hang out with your family. You have got to be kidding me!"

"It's for my grandparents' th anniversary. This only happens once. We need to go," I pleaded.

In retrospect, I realize what I was asking of my introverted husband was no small request. My large extended family had been such a big part of my childhood that I never considered the sizable, somewhat chaotic gathering would be a lot for someone who had little connection to most of the people who would be there. Torn by my desire to honor my husband's wishes and my preference to see my aunts and uncles and cousins, I continued making plans for the trip. Eventually, he relented.

The next hiccup in the trip for us was lodging. At the time I was the only married grandchild. And for the first time my parents, aunts, and uncles had to figure out how to accommodate more than just their immediate family concerns. Since I am nearly years older than my youngest cousin, ours was a family dynamic that was going to be in constant flux for quite some time. It had been confirmed there were enough beds for everyone who was traveling to Fort Robinson, but it was not confirmed if there were enough bedrooms for all of the married couples in the family. When I pressed for more information, I was told the only accommodation left available to Jeff and me was a bunk bed...and we would probably have to tolerate cousins in the room with us as well.

Nope. No way. That wasn't happening.

We had only been married for months. I was a second-year teacher at a Lutheran high school, and Jeff was still working at a job that paid just above an intern hourly wage without paid vacation. We would have to travel alone and be expected to pay our fair share for the lodgings. It was going to be a budget stretch to start with, and it was the only vacation we were getting for another year. Being forced to sleep in bunk beds would have been bad enough. But to be asked to share a room with my sisters and younger cousins, therefore foregoing needed alone time after hours with family and several days of opportunities for newlywed vacation sex, added insult to injury. It also did nothing to increase Jeff's level of enthusiasm for the entire venture.

There had to be another option.

When we discovered the state park also had a campground a fair distance from the historical buildings where the rest of the family would be staying, that settled it. We would take our tent, camp away from everyone and everything, and still have our own space at the end of each day.

Then we decided to complicate our own matters by expanding our family immediately before taking the trip.

As soon as we received news of our accepted house offer, we started looking at puppies. Jeff had multiple dogs throughout his childhood, and I had finally gotten over the fear of dogs that sent me running away from my Michigan grandparents' large German Shepherds. If I was going to venture into dog ownership, I wanted a Siberian Husky, a breed I had always admired from a distance. Their wolf-like appearance, soft fur, and the possibility of blue eyes were everything I wanted in a puppy. And Jeff was happy to oblige if it meant we were adding a dog to our family.

We selected our new puppy before we closed on our house, and then had to wait several more weeks before she was ready to leave her mom. We named her Sierra, after my love for mountains, and brought our furball home just weeks before we were set to take our trip. She was too young to board at a kennel for a week, and we didn't want to leave her training to anyone but us. So we did what any self-respecting -something childless couple would do: we took her out west with us.

Jeff and I split the driving distance in half, stopping to visit some of my college friends in Seward, Nebraska, and giving our puppy plenty of stops to stretch and pee along the way. We swore we would force her to sit in the area behind the front bench of our Ford Ranger, well aware that allowing her to sit in the front with us would lead to a lifetime of struggling to keep her in the backseat of any vehicle. But she quickly proved to be too fluffy, too cuddly, and too cute to leave anywhere but our laps. We would pay dearly for that lack of self-control in the years to come.

After two days of travel across the Midwest, we arrived in the northwest corner of Nebraska at dusk. We drove our truck across the small creek separating the campground from the rest of the park, then set up our base camp and temporary refuge from my extended family.

Looking back, the parent in me can see the allure of Fort Robinson State Park. It is Nebraska's largest state park with a lodge, cabins, and a lot of different outdoor activities. After years of camping around the country, I now know of several other state parks that would have offered the same amenities and been significantly closer to most of the family. But Nebraska is woven into my dad's family's DNA. The state was just one of many places where my grandfather served as a pastor, his large brood of seven in tow. My grandfather, dad, and several aunts and uncles went to Concordia University in Seward, Nebraska. Then I became the first grandchild of many to follow in their footsteps.

Over the course of the next couple of days, Jeff and I helped with our assigned meals and participated in activities with my cousins, aunts, and uncles. My cousin Kristen and I tipped our canoe at least once during a trip down a narrow, muddy creek, the two of us giggling like school girls at each upset. Jeff went golfing with my dad, uncles, and one aunt.

And then Jeff won over the majority of my aunts when he showed them just why I fell in love with him in the first place.

Even before I knew I wanted to marry him, I knew Jeff would be a good dad someday. When our relationship got serious and Jeff introduced me to his extended family, I fell even more in love with him as I watched him play with his younger cousins. And as always happened when Jeff saw his cousins, the same thing happened with my youngest relatives. He was attacked by a pile of little boys and girls as soon as he entered the pool to play. And play he did. My aunts, the mothers of the children who had found a willing playmate, looked over at me then and confirmed what I had known all along: I had a keeper.

During the several days we spent at Fort Robinson, we enjoyed time with my extended family, snuggled with Sierra, and let my younger cousins pet and play with her. And every night we returned to our home base, away from the loud and potentially intrusive company of family so we could be alone in our own tent, just the three of us.

Where camping had previously been a way for us to get out of the confines of our home for a weekend outside, camping at Fort Robinson gave us the space we needed to escape the family chaos after a long day of conversations, activities, and the constant clamor of my little cousins' hunger for more time with my good-natured husband.

Once the reunion was over and we packed up our equipment, we made the long haul straight home to Indiana. To break up the drive, we made a few stops along the way, including a quick break at Carhenge, a replica of Stonehenge constructed with vintage cars painted gray.[2] There wasn't much to see as we made the rest of our way back to I-80 and headed east, but we made the best of the hours together in the car.

And during the course of the trip, our fluffy little puppy, who would eventually grow to be fifty pounds of pure fur, joyously sat on our laps for nearly 2,000 miles. She mastered the art of walking on a leash every time we stopped to stretch our legs. And she learned that

---

2. I couldn't resist the opportunity to see a replica of the original stone structure, which I had seen four years earlier while I was studying in London.

sleeping in her small crate in our tent gave her the closeness with her people she desired every night.

Just like me, Sierra was hooked.

Chapter 6
Our Camping Dog

From day one, Sierra was a camping natural. And because we would remain childless for the first seven years of our marriage, she was central to most of our early camping excursions.

Our first house didn't have a backyard, so Sierra spent the first two years of her life becoming accustomed to a tie-out and leash when she needed potty breaks or when we took her on much-needed walks. I remember one night in particular, immediately following a growth spurt, when I pulled on the line and discovered only a busted collar, but no dog. She panicked as she realized she was collarless and without the security of a line that kept her close to our house. I tried not to laugh as she chased down her collar and waited for me to put it safely around her neck again.

In many ways, Sierra was the anti-husky. Our research before bringing her home informed us Siberian Huskies are notorious escape artists. They find any and every way to get out of a penned-up situation. But our Sierra never tried to escape. When we moved to Indianapolis and finally had a fenced-in yard, she never once attempted to leap over the three-foot fence—even though her jumps to greet every visitor who came to our home made it perfectly clear she could have easily run away if she wanted to.

It wasn't just her lack of desire to escape that made her the perfect camping dog. The only time she ever *really* wanted to be outdoors was when she was with us. Again, the anti-husky. She never complained about being attached to the line we had to put out at our campsite to keep her a reasonable distance from other dogs. She willingly went into her crate if we were going to leave for an errand or if we were going to a rare location where she would not be welcome. She rarely barked or paid attention to other dogs if they went past, often feigning a sort of bored disinterest in what they were doing. She was an outdoor princess, and she refused to let others ruffle her feathers, one of her few truly husky traits.

In our early years of marriage, I was a notoriously bad cook. But I could rock the camping breakfast, especially with the cast iron cookware we had gotten for a steal at Sam's Club. Even when it was just the two of us humans, I would make bacon and eggs and occasionally branched out to make pancakes from scratch. Once we had eaten all we could, we would give the rest to Sierra. She gobbled up any leftovers, but her favorite treats were pancakes. She would take the extra pancakes after she'd eaten her fill and delicately bury the leftovers with her nose, covering her snout in dust and barely hiding the discarded breakfast. Then she'd proudly prance over to us, as if she knew a secret no one else could possibly be a party to.

The first time we saw her doing this, we couldn't stop laughing. Suddenly the video we had taken of her using her nose to "bury" her leftover dog food into the middle of her dog pillow made a lot more sense. This was just how she saved food for later.

Until our daughter was born six years later, Sierra was as integral to our camping stories as we were. She joined us on hikes and settled right into the leaves and dirt of each new campsite. Camping meant she could join us on vacation instead of being left with strangers. It was hard to imagine camping without her. It was hard to imagine our *lives* without her.

Chapter 7
A Perfect Trip to Yellowstone

THERE WERE ONLY A few times we had to leave Sierra behind, like when she stayed with my in-laws the summer after our trip to Nebraska. It didn't make sense to invest in travel plans at first. I was going to be teaching summer school for the first few weeks of the summer and I had accepted that we would spend our third married summer at home, settling on weekend trips up to Michigan or day trips into Chicago if we got really adventurous.

But then Jeff threw me a curveball in early June.

"Let's go to Yellowstone."

I was speechless at first. "You mean, like, Yellowstone National Park? In Wyoming?"

"Yeah, I've never been."

Suddenly I had a million questions. "You know that Yellowstone is one of the most popular national parks in the country, right? People reserve lodging a year in advance. Do you honestly think we can find a place to stay *now*? There isn't much time to plan. And do we really have the money to go? I mean, a trip like that won't be cheap."

"Sure it will. We could camp."

The remaining questions whirling in my head suddenly stopped. Now there was something I had never considered before.

I had been to Yellowstone National Park only once before. When I was twelve, my maternal grandparents flew out from Michigan to visit us in Wyoming, and on the top of my grandmother's wish list was a trip to Yellowstone. So our family of six traveled several hours north with my grandparents. We stayed for a few nights in park hotels while we drove around and visited the major sites.

Looking back, I remembered driving past forests recently destroyed by wildfires only a couple of years before. Tiny wildflowers blanketed the ground underneath charred tree trunks, and baby trees poked out of the earth, ready to grow and replace the pines that had gone up in smoke.

I remembered my photography-loving grandmother as she insisted we stop for every photo opportunity, her SLR tightly gripped in her hands. This included one particular incident when my mother chastised her for wanting to get out of the car so she could get a better picture of the bison that freely roamed the park.[1]

I remembered Old Faithful Lodge and the birth of a dream that someday I would be able to afford a room at the historic hotel and do more than just take photos on the porch.

And Jeff was giving me the opportunity to go back.

The truth was, the more I thought about traveling out west with my new husband, the more excited I became. And after dragging him all the way to western Nebraska the summer before, I honestly felt like Jeff deserved to pick the next big vacation. I decided I could make it work, so I dove into planning our cross-country trip.

When I calculated the cost of driving out there with our Ford Focus and the per-night fees of camping every night, I realized my summer school salary would more than pay for the trip, even with the week of lost wages for Jeff.[2] My first two years of teaching had been full of challenges, often disrupting our time together as the long hours forced me to come home late. Jeff was still working in Michigan, which meant he spent two hours on the road each day. We hadn't even been married for three years, but the tension between our per-

---

1. Dear reader, while it was funny at the time, do not attempt to get close to bison under any circumstances. They are large, they are fast, and they will kill you. It happens at least once a year in and around Yellowstone.

2. Jeff's evolving job as a production scheduler still didn't offer paid vacation time.

sonal and professional lives weighed heavily on us. The truth was, we needed a vacation for just the two of us.

So I mapped out our adventure. I calculated how far we could drive in a single day and still get to a campsite with enough time to set up our tent in daylight. We talked about the stops we wanted to make along the way and determined the only two sites Jeff really wanted to see were Mount Rushmore and Yellowstone. Anything else along the way would be a bonus.

With a 3,000-mile journey ahead of us, we knew we both had to make compromises. We carefully planned out our meals for the week. We froze all of our meat and some other food items so they could stay colder for longer in our five-day cooler. We combed through our camping supplies, deciding which items were absolutely necessary and putting all of the extra camping equipment we didn't think we would need back into storage. I printed out camping recipes and our reservation plans and maps.[3]

Then, the night before we hit the road, we drove Sierra up to Jeff's parents so she could spend the week with them. We had filled up the backseat of our Focus and didn't yet know what regular stops we'd be taking along the way. We also had concerns about taking Sierra around a park full of natural dangers to a dog that refused to walk a straight line. Ultimately, leaving her at home was the best option.

And then we drove from northwest Indiana to Yellowstone National Park and back in eight days.

It felt like the craziest thing we had ever attempted as a couple to that point. But after a few years of learning how to work as a camping team, we were ready. We headed north, driving through Minnesota and up to South Dakota.

We finally arrived in Sioux Falls before the sun started its decline in the west. Because we had a tent camping site, we were exiled to the far reaches of the campground, with a fence and a field behind us. We started the rhythm of making camp—setting up the tent, putting our

---

3. GPS wasn't an option for us in 2004.

sleeping gear inside, making dinner, relaxing for a couple of hours, then heading to bed so we could get up early and do it all over again.

As we got further west, Jeff saw the signs for Badlands National Park.

He turned to me from the driver's seat, grinning, "Want to drive through?"

"The Badlands?" The name sounded like something out of a classic western. It was a place I had never really considered as a destination or scenic route. "How far off of our drive is it?"

"It isn't. We're going right past it. We should at least check the visitor center."

So we took a turn and drove into the park.

They say beauty is in the eye of the beholder, but I don't necessarily believe that is true. To understand and appreciate beauty, we need to accept that it takes many forms. And that requires us to look past our noses to what is in front of us at any given moment. Growing up in Michigan with acres of woods, sand dunes, and large natural lakes only a few miles away, I had a difficult time accepting the desert lands of Wyoming as beautiful. But after living in central Wyoming for a few years, I learned to look up and let my eyes appreciatively sweep the horizon. I learned to look past the sagebrush-covered desert and toward the snowcapped mountains. I learned that one kind of beauty is not better than another; it's just a different part of creation.

The Badlands were given their title for a reason. There is nothing in this part of the map. No water, little vegetation, and a horizon that stretches for miles and miles.

But then I stopped to look, really look at the rock formations, canyons, and small peaks everywhere we turned. There was a clear blue sky as a backdrop. The sun beat down on us, and I couldn't believe I had actually considered just driving right past. At our stop in the visitor center, Jeff picked up a National Parks Passport Book. His older sister had one and he looked at me, a question in his eyes as to whether or not we should buy it. After all, this wasn't the only national park we were visiting on this trip.

"No," I said. "We don't need to spend our money on that. How many national parks do you think we're going to keep visiting?"

If I'd only known...

We finally got back in the car, well aware we had a camping site to get to by nightfall.

Then we approached Wall Drug.

After seeing signs for the tourist trap for hundreds of miles, we also stopped. I mean, didn't we *have* to stop? Can one truly say they have visited western South Dakota if they *haven't* stopped at Wall Drug?

We walked through all of the shops. We took obligatory silly pictures of a stuffed buffalo, a random T-rex, and an oversized jackalope. Then we kept going. We drove up to the grounds of Mount Rushmore National Monument in the late afternoon, just as the sun sat directly behind the mountain with four carved faces. We couldn't look without squinting our eyes. It was hot, and we had already had a long day. But we walked around, took pictures, read the signs, watched a few short documentaries inside the visitor center, and left.

I could sense Jeff's disappointment at this being his first visit to the national monument. It was hard to tell if it was a sign we were trying to do too much in one day, or if it was just never going to be a highlight in our trip.

We spent the night at a KOA, the two of us and our tent surrounded by the piney woods of the Black Hills.[4] There was a slight change in climate as the sky grew dark. The Midwestern summer humidity gave way to slightly drier air and cooler nights. It was perfect weather for camping in our dome tent.

Eager to make it to Yellowstone, we woke up the next morning ready to continue west. I initially suggested we take a detour and

---

4. KOA stands for "Kampgrounds of America," a national chain of privately owned campgrounds that have a known standard. For two newbies at camping travel, the website made for easy trip planning instead of searching for less expensive and more scenic options. It would take me years before I branched out and looked for a range of options for places to set up camp.

head up to Devil's Tower, the location of that ill-fated thunderstorm from my childhood. But Jeff pointed out we didn't have the time or energy for an extra stop. So we drove and drove, switching who was behind the wheel when the other person needed to stretch. Soon we were twisting up into the mountains, the winding highway taking us to the eastern entrance of Yellowstone National Park.

The problem? The sun was already setting through our west-facing windshield. We still had to drive through the entire park with squinted eyes to get to West Yellowstone, where I had made our camping reservation for the next four nights.

Needless to say, it was dark by the time we finished our lonely drive through the park. We lit a single propane lantern and began setting up our tent in the quickly dropping temperatures. When we had finally set up our sleeping quarters, I was able to make dinner, mostly thanks to the outdoor kitchens available to both tent and RV campers. The camp kitchen pavilions had stoves, sinks, and tables for eating prepared meals. I was thrilled at the discovery.

When we finally awoke the next morning, it was to cool, dry air and mountains in the distance. Even my husband, who loved spending his weekends sleeping in until late morning, was ready to get up and explore the park. We packed what food and water we had and eagerly drove back to the West Yellowstone entrance.

When I was a freshman in high school, my physical science teacher informed us we lived close enough to Yellowstone National Park that we would be immediately destroyed if the lava bubbling beneath the surface of the entire park would someday explode.[5] In the years since, I have never forgotten Yellowstone lies on top of a supervolcano. And

---

5. Yes, this was a real class at my high school. We took earth science one semester and physical science the next—basically elementary physics and chemistry.

those words from my freshman science teacher come up every time I teach a novel or short story that relates to a natural apocalypse.[6]

This time with Jeff, the knowledge about the volcanic activity bubbling beneath the surface made the sights, sounds, and smells of America's first national park even more incredible. We followed marked trails around boiling mud pots and multicolored springs ringed with mineral deposits. We stopped at powerful waterfalls and took pictures of geysers big and small. We marveled at the juxtaposition of boiling hot springs with the icy cold Yellowstone Lake sitting peacefully in the background, surrounded by the Rocky Mountains. We laughed at the lines of cars parked on the side of any road as passengers took pictures of wildlife. And then we sheepishly took our own pictures to help us remember every last detail once we returned home.

While the northeast portion of the park was blocked off due to road work, we still worked hard to make the best of our time in this giant new playground. But I realized my feelings about Yellowstone's lodge had changed with time. Sure, I fell back in love with the rustic woodwork, cathedral-height ceilings, and wide porch surrounding the lodge I'd loved in my childhood. But I didn't feel the need to stay there anymore. I had everything I needed in the domed tent we had made our home for the week.

After three days of exploring Yellowstone and promising each other we would someday return once we had kids in tow, we started the trek back to Indiana. We drove past the Grand Tetons and down toward Riverton, Wyoming, so I could show Jeff where my family had lived for five years. It's funny how much I remembered as I drove through the town, finding my way past the high school and the house my family had lived in for those five years. I drove past the cemetery

---

6. The super nerd in me got more excited than I should have been about teaching Cormac McCarthy's *The Road*, mostly because it gave me an excuse to teach AP Literature students about Yellowstone's volcanic potential. The dark, post-apocalyptic tale is far from my favorite book, but I enjoyed teaching it that one time.

to find the gravestone of one of my high school friends who had died the year after our family moved back to Michigan. Then we continued southeast, stopping at Hell's Half Acre, a 960-acre canyon in the middle of flat land that was one of our traveling landmarks every time my family drove from Riverton to Casper, Wyoming, when I was a kid. And finally we continued on toward Colorado.

When we made our plans to head west, Jeff's sister Kristen had suggested we find a way to meet up and camp for a single night before we headed all the way home. So we found one last KOA near a small town in southwest Wyoming and met her there, setting up camp and finishing off the last of the food that had made it all the way from Indiana without spoiling.[7] We were slowly emerging from a quiet vacation away from everyone and everything we knew, and Jeff and I were both glad to share in the short time with family.[8]

We finally worked our way to I-80, driving across Nebraska and Iowa in an attempt to make it all the way home in a single stretch—until we blew a tire. I don't handle changes to my plans very well, and roadside breakdowns tend to send me down a rabbit hole of worst-case scenarios. We were almost to Illinois, and after that, Indiana. We were so close to home, and I worried about the extra expense of a hotel room on top of the new tire. The unfortunate stop and extra expenditure were not the way we wanted to end our vacation. But we were still thankful we were close to an exit and got the tire fixed without too much trouble.

---

7. Many years later, during the month between the sale of our second camper and the purchase of our third camper, Jeff found pictures online of the very same KOA we had stayed at with his sister. We had vivid memories of a camp store building surrounded by open land and a campsite that backed onto real darkness once the sun went down. The pictures that excited campers had posted of fresh trailer pads and cleanly landscaped patches of grass didn't match the memories of the tent sites where we had parked for the night nearly fifteen years before.

8. With the exception of my sister Rachel, who also lives in the Indianapolis area, all of our other siblings live in different cities in different states.

For years, that trip was marked as the best vacation ever. We traveled down to Florida a couple of times with Jeff's family and we made good memories. But it wasn't the same as parking and hiking through the Badlands. We drove to Washington, D.C. and back so I could attend a conference before we explored local historical sites and national monuments. But the hotel in New Jersey wasn't the same as waking up together in our chilly tent and walking right outside to blue skies and snowcapped mountains.

Jeff and I were several years away from any kind of economic stability. In another year we would both be moving to new jobs that would transition us from barely paying the bills to lifelong stable careers. One of the biggest lessons we learned from our trek to Yellowstone was we didn't need to spend a lot of money to make lasting memories. My childhood had taught me the leanest vacations were usually the least exciting. But one week on the road traveling halfway across the country and back had taught me being lean was freeing.

This is why we keep delaying our return out west with our kids. Because we want to stop in the Badlands and hike through the park instead of just walking along the trails just outside of the visitor's center. We want to see Crazy Horse as the counterpart to Mount Rushmore and visit both before being blinded by the position of the sun. We want to stop at Devil's Tower so I can show my whole family the place where my camping career nearly ended. We want to show our kids a magical land where bison roam freely in the wild, water shoots out of the ground and pours over cliffs, mud bubbles and pops, and steam rises in front of an icy cold mountain lake.

It was a perfect trip, one I want to relive only when the time is right.

Chapter 8
Finding Parks in Indiana

By the time we returned from Yellowstone, Jeff and I felt like we could conquer the world. We saw ourselves as camping experts, road warriors. For the first time in my life, I believed I could face any challenge that nature threw at me—as long as Jeff was by my side.

But our next chapter didn't bring challenges from nature; it brought challenges from life.

In my second year of teaching, I took on the extracurricular responsibilities of co-directing both the fall and spring play at the small high school where I taught English. My teaching and directing responsibilities made justifying more than a short camping trip difficult. Plus there were the complications of me teaching in the far south side of Chicago and Jeff working in Michigan while we were living in northwest Indiana. We camped when we could, but real escape to the outdoors felt impossible.

In those early years of teaching, I allowed myself every excuse to not leave home for the weekend. I had grading to do and lessons to prepare. And in less than two years of marriage, we had purchased a house and adopted a dog. I tried to relax with friends and family when we did go camping, but I always seemed to have things to do. It was a rough three years full of too much work, too little support, and a near change in career. I just didn't know if I could keep up my teaching load without losing my marriage, myself, or both.

When I got the phone call for an interview at a school in Indianapolis, I jumped at the opportunity for a new job and a chance to start over together. Within several weeks I had accepted a new position. Soon Jeff also found a new job in Indianapolis, and we were finally living and working in the same city. It was a revolution for our relationship.

When we moved from the Chicago area to Indy, we entered a new camping territory paired with fresh challenges. My teaching schedule became significantly more manageable, but my extracurricular schedule became significantly more involved. I suddenly found myself relatively inexperienced and in charge of a much larger theater program than the one I'd co-led before. Young and idealistic, I poured most of my extra energy into both the spring and fall plays at the school. Weekends became packed with set building and choreography rehearsals, which made fall and early spring camping trips difficult. Jeff had to force me to get away when a free weekend appeared, mostly so we could focus on each other and forget the pressures of work. But once the weekend extracurricular responsibilities melted away each May, we immediately started looking for available weekends when we could get back out into nature.

One camping trip that quickly became a yearly tradition during our Indianapolis years was our early summer church campout. The church we joined in Indy included a sizable group of families that had been scheduling an annual weekend for camping and fellowship for a few years already. It was one more reason to feel at home in our new church. The first year we joined in the church campout fun, the organizers had selected Turkey Run State Park, just over an hour west of Indianapolis.

Our friend Steve, Jeff's Best Buy coworker from Grand Rapids, kept hinting he wanted to come down to visit us in Indiana. We invited him to join us for the weekend of camping and fellowship, and the three of us plus our dog Sierra set up camp in a large spot near a ravine. The woods provided the perfect amount of shade to keep our tents cool in the midday heat. We learned the whole group would gather for worship, but for most of the weekend, different groups broke off based on age and outdoor interests. We spent time cultivating friendships with a small number of people through one of our favorite activities. I couldn't get enough of hiking through ravines and woods, the state park defying everything I had always believed about Indiana's hills and cornfields.

We participated in our church campout over the next three years. After our first year at Turkey Run, the location changed to Starved Hollow State Park, which didn't offer all of the hiking and biking activities we enjoyed. But we still appreciated the time the camping trip gave us to get to know people at our church and force us to get away from the city for a weekend. The second year of the campout we convinced my sister Rachel and brother-in-law Joel, who had followed us to live in Indianapolis, to join us. What followed was three years of going with friends *and* family, an additional bonus.

Jeff and I spent the next four childless years hopping around the state whenever we could. But while we could theoretically spend as much time as we wanted camping, Jeff legitimately complained we didn't do it enough. As a young, overcommitted teacher, my spare time was scarce, and Jeff and our dog Sierra's desire to get back on the road often went unnoticed. Between teaching and directing, I could spend ten or more hours a day at school and then return for at least one day of the weekend to catch up on grading or work on a play production. I was torn between my desire to be the very best at my job and the need to get away and out of the city with my husband.

When I did decide to put aside the schoolwork for a couple of days so we could get away, Jeff and I discovered an Indiana we never knew existed. I had believed for my entire life that Indiana was nothing more than flat land, with occasional hilly interruptions, and lots of cornfields. While this isn't completely wrong, the hills and cornfields in southern Indiana get higher and steeper. The forests get thicker and less sporadic. And eventually, it feels like stepping into another world.

The first time we discovered this was on our church camping trip to Turkey Run. We hiked along the ravines and waterfalls and stepped over creek beds. Suddenly there was a lot more to Indiana than we'd ever known before.

Then Brown County State Park swept us off of our feet.

Somehow Jeff convinced me during the two months of a fall play production that I could take a weekend off in October and travel down to a new state park for a fall camping trip. It was peak season for autumn foliage in Brown County, and we had been told one of the best places to see fall colors in Indiana was in the Bloomington area. I've never been able to resist a good autumn campout, with campfires and s'mores and perfect weather for daytime hiking and evening cuddling, so I was in.

We drove down to the hills of southern Indiana, past harvested crops, and into a canvas of fall colors. The temperatures dropped as the fire pit right outside our tent roared to life.

Sierra embraced her husky roots. A happy indoor dog, she returned to puppy-like behavior in the cool, outdoor climate, her thickened coat hinting of winter and snow to come. She settled into the dirt, dead leaves and sticks clinging to her tail and belly as she created her own little weekend nest.

The next day we headed out for a hike, the temperatures climbing into the 70s, making for appropriate summer attire paired with our hiking boots. Sierra pranced on the end of her leash, sniffing at everything and anything that came across her path, pulling when she saw other people and dogs out exploring. We climbed stairs, stepped over tree roots, and stopped at overlooks to take in every angle of the trees.

Then we suddenly found ourselves on a hiking trail with our dog at the same time as a group of horseback riders. It quickly became clear that dogs and horses do not mix.

The trail guide looked right at us and said, "You need to get off the path."

We looked at the edge of the path, which quickly dropped off to a ravine. Confused, we asked, "Down there?"

The horses in front of us began to stomp their hooves and huff, getting increasingly skittish at the sight of Sierra's wolf-like appearance. So we slowly backed into the ravine, each step more steep than the one before. It was a tricky balance, trying to get to a safe place away from the group while not being so far off the path we wouldn't be able to climb back out. We felt guilty as one horse with a young girl on it got spooked anyway, threatening to take off before being stopped by the quick-thinking trail guide. We watched them continue to meander down the trail, the horses' back ends sway accompanied by more snorts and huffs. Finally, we climbed out to continue our own horse-free adventure—on a very different trail.

Sierra, oblivious to the mess she had just created, resumed her happy romp at the end of the leash.

Despite the unplanned hiking difficulties, we fell in love with the trails and the views in Brown County. We repeated that particular fall camping trip once more during our tent years, but then it would be years before we returned to the park.

When I take the time to look back through the camping experiences and memories of our twenties, I see a lot of happy and fulfilling experiences that helped us grow as a couple, but I wish we had done more. These were the moments I was forced to stop working for once and take time to just enjoy life. I couldn't think about all of the things I had to do; I had to just be. Without cell phones and hotspots to keep us connected to the Internet, those early camping trips helped me focus on rest, something my busy brain and body never did at home. And it helped me connect with my husband without outside distractions, changing our marriage for the better and preparing us for the challenges to come.

Chapter 9
End of an Era

BECAUSE WE STARTED OUT as tent campers, I believed we were always going to be tent campers. We had airy tents to keep us cooler in the summer and heavy sleeping bags to keep us warmer in the early spring and late fall. I loved waking up to the sound of birds stirring with the sunrise and the rumble of thunder in the distance when rain threatened to derail our weekend plans. Our lives were better because we camped. Tent camping was relatively cheap and had allowed us to explore places that were otherwise outside of our budget.

Over the years, whether we were alone or with friends, we would gather under our screen tent during all kinds of weather and make fun of people who used anything but tents. After all, if you were sleeping in something with hard sides, were you really camping?

Then we had kids.

Or at least, we started *trying* to have kids.

I had spent years watching families wrangle their little ones on weekend adventures, setting up safe areas for wandering toddlers while inserting tent poles and hammering stakes with a speed and agility that only another parent could truly appreciate. These super parents made camping with small children look so easy. Even the smallest walkers were able to load up tents with gear and participate in family activities.

When we bought our bigger tent less than three years into our marriage, we weren't quite ready for kids. And if I'm being really honest, *I* wasn't ready for kids. My first three years of teaching had been rough for me professionally, and it had brought unexpected challenges to our marriage. The job had asked too much of me and sucked a lot of the optimism I held for my teaching career.

Our move to Indianapolis gave me new life. And while I was still working too much and our marriage took more of a backseat to my job than it should have, I *loved* my new school and position. When Jeff's younger sister—who got married six months after us—announced she was pregnant with her first baby, we felt like we needed to consider having babies as well so they could have cousins close in age.

I wanted kids—I never doubted it. But I still wasn't sure I was ready to put the effort into trying to get pregnant. Still, I didn't want to wait until we were thirty before we became parents, so I agreed Jeff and I could stop trying to *not* get pregnant and see what happened.

A year later, we still weren't pregnant. Two years later we were finally telling friends and then, with their encouragement, started seeking help. Jeff had been ready to be a dad for years, but I was finally feeling the pangs of grief every time I watched a new baby get baptized at church or when we went camping and saw a couple struggling to wrangle their little ones. I was finally ready to snuggle my own little one. Eventually, my fertility specialist put me on a cocktail of fertility drugs in an effort to produce more, stronger eggs. Jeff and I were both hopeful it would work.

It was during the eighth summer of our marriage that we decided we needed a bigger weekend trip. We were convinced I would be pregnant soon. I made a reservation for three nights in Wisconsin near the Sparta-Elroy bike trail, hoping the three-day romantic weekend would be our last getaway as a childless couple before we were able to announce to the world that we were going to be parents.

We arrived at the campground in time to set up our tent before nightfall, but Jeff quickly pointed out it was right across the narrow road from a bog. Sleeping across the road from a mosquito nursery? Not a good start.

By nightfall, we found ourselves running from truck to tent to avoid being carried off by a swarm of mosquitoes. I tried to laugh it off with Jeff, but we both became increasingly agitated.

The next morning I walked to the bathroom and confirmed what the mild cramping had warned: my period started. I sat in the bathroom for a few extra minutes, wiping away tears and trying to pull myself together. But my body was pumped full of synthetic and natural hormones, and as I flushed the toilet, I realized this *wouldn't* be our last trip as a childless couple.

As I returned from the bathroom, I held back more tears. I didn't want to tell Jeff. He had been hoping for this longer than me. He was so ready to be a dad and I felt like I was failing, again. The words bubbled out of me when our eyes met. "It didn't work." Immediately he understood. He wrapped me into a hug, took a long moment to soothe both of our hurt, and then took charge.

Determined to distract both of us from another month of disappointment, he rushed me into the truck so we could get on our way. We spent the day riding our bikes up and down the Elroy-Sparta trail. It became clear very quickly that we were out of shape and had no business biking the trail. But it was the temporary distraction we needed from another month without a positive pregnancy test.

It was dusk by the time we returned to the campground. In the headlights, we could see a swarm of mosquitoes guarding the entrance to our tent. When we finally settled in for the night, we had a decision to make. Jeff and I had never cut a camping trip short. We had suffered through rain, cold, and uncomfortable heat. Once we staked our tent down, we were committed for the time we had paid for. But this wasn't a typical pest problem. This was a mosquito army ready to attack without hesitation. And it was compounding what was already an emotionally charged weekend.

So we decided we were done.

The next morning, we went to the office and told the campground staff we were leaving a day early. Still on a very tight financial budget, I asked if we could have our money back for the last night, especially since we were leaving early because of the campsite conditions.

The manager sighed in response and said, "Well, some people just aren't cut out for camping."

And that was the thing that broke me.

My mind spun. *Excuse me? We aren't cut out for camping? We survived a premarital bout of altitude sickness and still kept camping. We traveled from Indiana to Yellowstone National Park with the bare minimum of our camping supplies, setting up our tent and taking it down every day, sometimes in the dark with just a single propane lantern throwing shadowed light on our progress. And we did the whole trip in eight days. We chased off hungry raccoons and thwarted them from taking our food out of our storage locker. We survived a thunderstorm on the sandy shores of Lake Michigan and kept camping even though water got through the floor of our tent, leaving puddles at our feet as we climbed out of our bed.*

We had spent eight years camping together, making the best of each situation. I hadn't perfectly handled every situation, but this felt different. I wasn't surrendering to nature; I wanted nature to give me a break.

But we had no idea what nature had in store for us.

Chapter 10
Kids Change Everything

As I watched the ultrasound technician dig around my uterus and fallopian tubes in early August, I could already tell she would give me another dose of bad news. This time around, none of the eggs were good enough to justify giving me the prescribed HCG shot. We would have to wait for further instructions from our doctor.

That was it. Three months of treatment and it hadn't worked. I held back the tears in the elevator as I rode down to the first floor. I was determined to not let strangers know I had just been crushed by the cold reality of a black and white screen.

I had squeezed in my appointment in the early morning hours before a back-to-school faculty meeting. I had told Jeff he didn't need to go with me to my routine appointment. He was supposed to leave for work in a matter of minutes and I was thirty minutes from home. I thought about calling him, but by the time I sat down in the driver's seat, I was sobbing. I didn't have the ability to speak. I sent him a text to stay at home and made the questionable decision to drive home on the I-465 loop through morning rush hour traffic.

When I finally made it home, I collapsed into Jeff's arms, trying to explain what had happened at the doctor's office. He held me tight, let me cry, and then tucked me back into bed with our dog Sierra before leaving for work. As he turned to leave our bedroom, I could see the hurt in his own eyes. "Sarah, we'll figure this out. It's not over."

I eventually got back up, washed my face, and pulled myself together for long enough to sit through faculty meetings, trying to focus on getting ready for a new school year. But my every thought was consumed with, "Now what?"

It was finally time to tell more people about our fertility struggle, and not just our closest friends. I told a couple of girlfriends the latest development so I could keep them in the loop. I sent an email to our parents, grandparents, and siblings to tell them everything we knew. I asked for prayers and support as we contemplated the next step. Finally, I sat down with my principal and told him I would very possibly need time off in the next couple of months as we looked into more aggressive treatments.

And then we waited. We waited for word from the doctor who was waiting for word from me that my next period had started so we could discuss new medication and timing. We waited to start an at-home shot regimen, the very idea petrifying to me.

Three weeks after my appointment, irritation set in. Nothing was happening, and I was tired of my body not behaving. Somehow, I convinced myself that taking a pregnancy test would finally get things started, so I woke up on a Saturday morning, took the test, put it on the counter, and went back to bed. I had seen the words "Not Pregnant" far too many times before. I had no interest in seeing them again.

A couple of hours later Jeff woke me up, pregnancy test in hand. "Did you look at this?"

I rolled over to look at him. "Why would I look at that? I know what it says."

"No seriously, look at it."

Something in his voice forced me to sit up and focus on the little test's screen. Instead of "Not Pregnant", the words clearly said, "Pregnant."

"How?" I mean yes, the nurse had told me there was a *possibility* my eggs would mature but to not count on it. And yes, I knew *how*, but we had been told it was a near improbability.

By this time we were practically buying stock in pregnancy tests. Three pregnancy tests later, Jeff and I were convinced. We were shocked and thrilled and unsure of what to do next. Within hours we had told one friend, my sister Rachel, and then another set of friends when they came over for dinner that night.

I was going to be a mother, and the reality of our changed future consumed my every thought for the next nine months.[1]

We didn't know it the previous July, but we would only use that tent one more time as a family.

Our daughter Lydia was born the following April. And while I was physically and emotionally exhausted from new motherhood, I was determined to try camping for the first time with our infant daughter on our church's annual camping trip.

That June, we packed up the car with all of our camping equipment and baby supplies. Jeff couldn't wait to share the magic of campfires and sleeping outdoors with our two-month-old. He was convinced this was going to be the beginning of a beautiful camping future for our baby girl, but I wasn't so sure. Lydia never took to breastfeeding, which meant I had spent the past two months struggling to pump and mix formula to keep our baby healthy. My labor had been difficult and I had episiotomy scars that still refused to completely heal. My body didn't feel like my body anymore and I couldn't begin to comprehend what it would be like to attempt hiking or even swim in Starved Hollow's small inland lake without feeling gross and out of shape. And I was *so* tired.

---

1. Funny enough, we were huge fans of *Scrubs*. When Carla got pregnant for the first time and Turk found out first, surprising her with the news, I told Jeff that would never happen. It was too ridiculous. And then it happened to us.

It wasn't a *complete* failure. I got some exercise. My sister and brother-in-law were more than happy to spend time holding their new niece and goddaughter. I handled middle-of-the-night feedings while I sat precariously on the edge of our air mattress, trying to keep our hungry, crying baby from waking up the neighbors. I changed diapers on the blanketed ground. I enjoyed the fellowship but was too tired to stay up late by the fire with friends and my sister.

But I wasn't ready to go out and try it again.

So I decided that for the time being, I was done with camping. I didn't want to discuss camping up in Michigan during our summer travels. I didn't want to talk about exploring Indiana state parks with our baby. I didn't want to talk about fall camping plans, even though I wouldn't be directing my school's fall play and I would have more free time.

Instead, we took a late summer trip to Pigeon Forge and Gatlinburg in Tennessee. With Lydia strapped to my chest in her infant carrier, we introduced her to trails and waterfalls and the black bears that climbed along the mountainsides.

Life never really stopped moving after that. On my 30th birthday, Jeff told me about the possibility of his job being transferred to Fort Wayne. Then I started graduate school in our new city and quickly got pregnant with our son. Then we bought a fixer-upper and gutted our house, working our way from room to room until there were places for our toddler to play safely and our soon-to-be-infant to sleep. We ended up having to replace an HVAC system and a well pump. Everything about our lives was a mess. Needless to say, the camping equipment moved with us—but it sat untouched in our new garage for the next year.

When I was two weeks away from my due date with our son Ethan, Jeff packed up our tent, pack-and-play, and toys and took two-year-old Lydia back down to central Indiana to go camping with our old church group. I was a mess of nerves at the possibility I would go into labor while my husband was at least three hours away, but ultimately I reveled in the calm before the storm. I enjoyed the break from being both a student and teacher and the two months off from researching and paper writing and grading. I cleaned our house one more time to the best of my ability in my very pregnant body. And our daughter appreciated one more weekend as an only child with some quality Daddy time.

But more importantly, that weekend helped Jeff see what camping with our little ones could look like. While I sat at home in the air conditioning and slept alone in our king-sized bed, he watched our daughter dig in the dirt and sit next to the campfire and enjoy life outside, bug bites and all.

Years before, when we were young and idealistic, we had purchased our upgraded tent with plans for adding a pack-and-play next to Sierra's crate, certain that with the addition of human children, we would continue as if nothing about our lives had changed.

Except, children change *everything*. The life you thought you would have turns upside down. And while those changes can bring great joy and fulfillment, it also requires us parents to adjust our dreams a bit.

Jeff just needed to help me see how to dream differently through our changed reality.

Chapter 11
"We're More the Camper Buying People"

AFTER SUFFERING THROUGH AN awkward timeshare pitch, we sat inside the salesman's office. Jeff and I were in the Smoky Mountains again, this time sans children to celebrate our tenth anniversary. Like many who travel with limited budgets, we figured a two-hour presentation was worth a free visit to the Titanic Museum in Pigeon Forge. I wrote a paper about the sinking during my first semester of college, Jeff had taken me to see *Titanic* when we were eighteen-year-olds still pretending we weren't dating, and Jeff appreciated history *almost* as much as me. It was one of the few indoor attractions we could agree on, so we went to the presentation.[1]

Our salesman tried. He pointed out all of the fun places we could visit with our small children, highlighting the possibility of international travel, beach vacations, and access to endless resorts anywhere we could want to travel. But we had stretched every dollar to make this every-five-years-as-a-couple vacation a possibility. I had no idea how he thought we would be able to afford these fun locations on top of the monthly payments to keep the timeshare in our possession.

I looked at Jeff. Jeff looked at the salesman. Finally, he said, "Actually, we're more the camper-buying type of people."

Jeff had been hinting at his desire to upgrade to a camper for years. He frequently mentioned his childhood memories with his family of

---

1. Yes, Dollywood would have been fun, but our anniversary is in December. We needed indoor activities.

six squeezed into a small camper. For a whole host of reasons—money, time, space, exhaustion—I kept ignoring his vocal daydreams. I was still in graduate school, working part-time as a graduate teaching assistant and part-time as a high school English teacher. We had a toddler and an infant. Our house still needed major renovations, including two bathrooms and a kitchen. The last thing I wanted to do on the weekends was pack up our small children and camping equipment. And we didn't have the time or money to consider any variety of RV.

But at that moment, I knew. Eventually, we would purchase a camper. Jeff had finally said it out loud to someone outside of our family, and I hadn't objected. I wanted my kids to love hiking and biking and campfires. I wanted to take them to national parks and show them the incredible natural diversity across the United States. I wanted them to appreciate the planet they live on and be eager to explore the outdoors instead of expensive experiences curated for the comfort of tourists.

Jeff and I returned from the trip and jumped right back into life as busy, working parents of two small children. I kept dreaming about the places I wanted to go and the things I wanted to see as a family and somehow Jeff had reminded me those dreams included camping again. We both wanted our kids, who had always been city kids and would most likely always be city kids, to experience more than daily exposure to a concrete jungle.

But I didn't know exactly how to find it again. Our world wasn't slowing down any time soon. We were broke. Our house needed work and every spare penny we had was going into paying off debt and fixing the next problem that arose.

Jeff had made it clear that his solution to getting our family back around a campfire was buying a camper. But I struggled to get past the idea that we would only *really* be camping if we did it in a tent. Tent camping helped us grow as a couple. I loved so many things about sleeping in a tent. There were also things I loathed: trying to stay dry when it rains all weekend, failing to find warmth when the fire won't light, and hot, humid nights from which there is no escape. The tent cities that couples with small children set up on their campsites had always impressed me. I knew how much work it was to do with just the two of us. Memorable? Yes. Cheap? YES! But it was still work and I couldn't imagine how much harder it would be with our two energetic, yet loveable, little ones.

And so, I once again made Jeff put camping dreams on the back burner. Eventually, he stopped making camping suggestions again and instead started secretly looking for available campers he thought we could afford.

With one year of graduate school left, I quit my part-time teaching assistant position to once again become a full-time high school teacher. We began paying off our debts from moving to a new city during the housing market crash. We took a financial planning class through our church. I finally learned how to budget our finances to calculate what we were spending and how much we were allowed to spend in a given month.

Through each step toward stability, I wondered why it took me until my mid-s to figure out that important life skill.

I'd spent my entire childhood painfully aware of how little my parents had; I had hoped my future would be different. But despite our two-income household, a combination of poor decisions and bad luck kept us spinning. I desperately wanted to not panic about every expense, to have the freedom to go out on dates without worrying about the expense of dinner *and* paying the babysitter, and to have a savings account with enough money for small emergencies.

The road to financial stability was a long journey. First, we replaced our Ford Ranger with a leased red F-150 shortly after our son was born. After ten years of truck ownership, our family had finally outgrown our little truck. The lease became the most practical solution to our most immediate problem: needing two vehicles that could easily transport two children.

With the truck, Jeff had more freedom to dream. He took me to the camper show in Fort Wayne two years in a row, giving me a glimpse of what could be. Then Jeff started seriously looking at used campers. I argued we needed to be able to pay with cash because we couldn't take on *more* debt. He countered we didn't have time to wait for cash. Our kids were moving out of the toddler years. If we wanted to enjoy quality time with them in the outdoors, we either needed to get out our tents or buy a camper with payments we could afford. Finally, I relented.[2] Quality family togetherness, exposure to new experiences, and precious memories trumped being debt-free for me.

We went from hypothetical camper owners to seriously looking for a family-friendly camper in just a few months. Always concerned about finances, I initially looked at pop-ups, convinced it would still be easier than setting up and taking down a tent while giving us the option of heating and air-conditioning. Jeff became enamored with hybrids. They would give us a smaller footprint in our driveway than a full travel trailer but would give us more space inside than a smaller pop-up, the hard sides providing us the option of a small bathroom. We looked at every used camper option available to us, even considering going from having nothing at all to purchasing a large travel trailer at a solid used price.[3]

Finally, we found the hybrid trailer we felt was right for our family at a price I could justify. Now that I had leveled up my budgeting skills, I determined we could easily pay it off in a couple of years.

Our Rockwood Roo hybrid had a small slide-out with a couch that gave us a sitting area across from our dining table, a kitchenette, plus

---

2. Living debt-free was a worthwhile goal and one we didn't plan to discard, but we also weren't willing to throw away quality family time while our kids were little. If we could find a way to make it work without becoming a burden, we would. We continue to stand by that decision.

3. We sometimes wonder what would have happened if we had purchased that larger camper right away. In the years since, I've seen a lot of camper renovations that have convinced me we could have made it work for several years. But at the time, I didn't know enough about the world of camper ownership to even try.

a full-sized bunk on one end and a queen bunk on the other.[4] The camper also had an outdoor stove to do all of our cooking outside without heating up the interior of the camper. One of the selling points of getting a camper was we would now have a built-in refrigerator, instead of a cooler, for travel. The camper had both air conditioning and heating, which meant we no longer had to worry about uncomfortable summer or late fall temperatures. It would not only get us out of town, but it would expand our spring, summer, and fall options regardless of climate conditions.

Most importantly, we saw our camper purchase as our ticket to getting our kids out into nature. It was something we all needed, and we couldn't wait to give them the first camping experience they could both remember.

---

4. For those uninitiated, a slide-out remains inside the camper while it is in storage and then is rolled out with motors once the camper is parked in a camp site. It increases the size of a camper by moving some of the interior space outward.

Chapter 12
"We Could Camp"

JEFF SHEEPISHLY LOOKED UP at me from his cell phone. "So next summer is the 150th anniversary of the battle of Gettysburg. How cool would it be to go?"

He had his history-loving wife's full attention. "Um, yes, please. That would be amazing!" Then I hesitated. "What about the kids? They wouldn't get anything out of it."

Jeff grinned, a wink in his voice as he said, "I wasn't talking about a family trip. Just the two of us."

It had been over a year since our trip to the Smoky Mountains. My brain started buzzing with travel plans and questions. "Everything has to already be booked for that big of an event, doesn't it?"

Jeff saw his opportunity. "We could camp."

When he'd said that nine years before, we ended up in Yellowstone National Park. The last three years of our lives had been in a spiral. I couldn't wrap my mind around Jeff's sudden sense of adventure, but I also wanted to finally return to Gettysburg to see the full glory of the park over a few days.[1]

I took a deep breath. "Okay, I'll find us a campsite."

---

1. I alluded to it earlier, but in 2006 we stopped in Gettysburg on the way back from a summer conference trip to D.C. and then a two-day stop in Philadelphia. We arrived at the national military park an hour before it closed, got our national park passport stamped, and then attempted to drive the long tour through the battlefields. We got about two-thirds of the way through the tour before the sunset, and then we started driving home to Indiana.

And that is how our maiden camper voyage became a couple's trip to Gettysburg. At first, I believed he just wanted to get out the tents, but Jeff had a master plan to get me back into camping, and a camper was part of it. Slowly, he convinced me the added advantage of air-conditioning during the Fourth of July weekend in the Pennsylvania mountains would make the weekend trip even more enjoyable.

I had selected a site for our large tent. I wasn't concerned about room for a 20-foot-long hybrid because we didn't own one when I made the reservations. I made several frantic phone calls to the campground to ensure our new camper would fit on our site. By the second phone call, I realized I wasn't going to believe them until I saw it with my own eyes.

And then we prepared to hit the road.

The trailer sat parked in our driveway when I got back from driving up to Michigan to drop the kids off with their grandparents. For the first time in four years, I was truly excited about the possibility of camping again.

While I was driving to Michigan and back, Jeff had started moving all of our camping equipment from the back of our garage. Each item, from lanterns to cast iron cookware, brought back a flood of memories. Within hours, tools that had been sitting around for the better part of three years found a new home and the hint of a new adventure.

Since we would be leaving in the late afternoon, we decided to camp in Ohio for our first night. And I almost derailed our romantic getaway within hours of our departure. As part of my planning for the trip, I had looked up every national park location between Fort Wayne and Gettysburg, discovering Cuyahoga Valley National Park in Ohio on our way to our first camping spot. Google Maps gave me directions to the national park, but it took us through a civilized area with no clear indication of how to find the national park visitor center. Our GPS was still not sophisticated enough to help. And I willfully ignored my husband's anxiety over towing our camper for the very first time.

"Sarah, where are you taking us?" He tried to keep his irritation at bay, but he wasn't succeeding.

"The directions say it's right around here. See, look at that sign. We should be able to get our stamp in that parking lot!"

It was a small parking lot. Jeff was towing an extra 20 feet behind us, and there was no sign of the visitor center anywhere.

Jeff sighed. "Sarah, this is ridiculous. We need to keep going."

Disappointed and a bit chagrined, I didn't argue. It wasn't worth the additional tension in our truck. So it became the stamp stop that wasn't, and he's never let me forget it.

Grimacing, Jeff continued the drive and we arrived at a private campground well before dark, where we set up our camper and started to learn a new camping routine. We went from tent experts to camper rookies. We let down the bunks, connected the water and electric, made our bed, and then I started making dinner on our outdoor stove. For the first time in a long time, it was quiet. No screaming children. No blaring TV. No technology pings. I relaxed. I had forgotten what it was like to finally be forced out of the house.

Everything was perfect—until we crawled into bed.

I heard a creak as I crawled across to the far side of the bed. Then Jeff crawled in behind me.

CRACK

We felt the jolt as the bunk dropped on Jeff's side. Quickly, we scrambled out of the bed, running outside to inspect the issue. While we had checked everywhere for potential water damage in our new-to-us camper, we hadn't seen the rot under the bigger of the two bunks. It had been hidden by the frame—until the frame broke.

Then the nervous laughter started. I was relieved we hadn't fallen through our camper in the middle of the night. Jeff was relieved we were both still clothed when it happened. So we closed the queen bunk, pushing in the bulge from where the mattress pushed out the metal frame, and we promptly headed over to the full-bed-sized bunk intended for our kids.

The issue was fixed with a quick call to our salesperson when we got home. And the rebuilt bunk was solid, but for the rest of the summer I cautiously crept into bed—and every time I breathed a sigh of relief when the bed remained solid beneath me.

The next day, we traveled across the Pennsylvania mountains. I convinced Jeff to make more history stops at the Johnstown Flood National Memorial and the Flight 93 Memorial. Neither were romantic in nature, but this was a trip that fed the history nerd in both Jeff and me more than anything.

With daylight to spare, Jeff pulled into the private campground in Pennsylvania where we were staying for the next three nights. I had no idea what to expect. I didn't know if we would fit and neither of us had any idea how we would get into the site.

If tent building had been one of the first tests of our marriage, camper parking would test us in our second decade of marriage. The whole disastrous ordeal nearly ruined our mini-vacation before we had a chance to see Gettysburg.

"Turn this way!" I shouted from the front of our campsite.

Jeff's jaw clenched. "What way?"

"To the passenger side. No stop! There's a tree. Now you're going to go into the ditch!"

"I can't turn it that fast. And if you can't see my mirrors, I can't see you!"

In short, it wasn't going great.

I had no idea which direction to tell Jeff to turn or how to communicate with him the best way to do so. The site had a small gully and several trees and Jeff finally disconnected the camper, changed angles, and then reconnected to get going in the right direction. He got frustrated with me; I got frustrated with my inability to help him. And then I got frustrated with him for not understanding I didn't know what I was doing.

To be honest, I wish I could say I've gotten better about helping my husband with difficult parking jobs. But he's just gotten better at figuring out how to park our camper while I run back and forth and attempt to communicate with him what he needs to do next. But at least now we're able to laugh about our first trip out.[2]

When we were finally parked, I was thankful Jeff had talked me into the camper before our trip. The July temperatures had peaked in the 90s with high humidity. Our original plan included a tent with fans. Our new plan included an air conditioner.

I could finally fully accept our decision to become one of "those" people who "camp" without a tent.

The next day we parked at the Gettysburg Visitor Center, where we explored the new museum. Then we caught a shuttle to the George Spangler Farm Civil War field hospital site, the location of one of many field hospitals in the weeks and even months following the battle.

Despite the heat, we did what we had been dreaming about doing since the moment we started planning the trip: we followed the motor tour using our bikes instead of our truck. It allowed us to get up close and personal with the battlefields in a way that we never could from the comfort of our air-conditioned vehicle. We had both spent the past six months getting into the best shape of our lives. I had finally lost all of the baby weight from both pregnancies, and we were ready to put our physical fitness to the test.

There were a couple of things that struck me the first time we visited Gettysburg in a race against the sunset. One, I never understood the Battle of Gettysburg happened *in* the town of Gettysburg. Yes, most of the fighting took place in the surrounding fields, but there was this sleepy little town suddenly in the middle of a battle many consider to be the turning point of the Civil War. Second, I didn't realize the scope of the battlefields, the vastness of the area that the Union had to defend and the Confederate army had to attack.

---

2. When we took a family trip to Gettysburg in the summer of 2022, we wanted to find that first site and see if it was as bad as we remembered. But we didn't have the time to stop at a completely different campground.

I began to understand the size and scope then, but our 16-mile bike ride brought those realities home.

We made it back to our truck, exhausted, sweaty, hungry, dehydrated, and ready to crash. We drove past the one stop we did not get to on our bikes, but I couldn't get myself out of the truck to see the view from Culp's Hill.

Jeff declared he wanted a lazy morning the next day. But much to my husband's chagrin, I was up to make bacon and eggs at 8 AM. It had been years since I had made a true camping breakfast. And while my cooking had improved considerably since our kids had been born, I still prided myself in making a mean breakfast with our cast iron skillet. At the smell of my prepared feast, Jeff relented to eating breakfast before preparing to head out for another day of exploration.

We walked and shopped down the main drag in Gettysburg on our second day. Even with the thousands of tourists every year, the historical town has maintained its charm. We found some fun local stores where we could buy gifts for the kids and ate lunch at a local restaurant. Then we managed to find a gift shop that was still selling reenactment tickets so Jeff could knock off one of his personal bucket list items. We spent the afternoon walking around the encampments, booths, and watching the 40-minute reenactment of the Wheatfield, the bloodiest fighting of the three-day battle of Gettysburg.

We wrapped up our trip with a campfire and the next morning headed all the way home. Jeff's parents met us at our house so we could see our kids again before putting them into bed. As I tucked both kids into bed, I realized Jeff had been right. We needed the camper.

Now it was time to see how the kids would respond to camping.

Chapter 13
"We Kept Returning to the Outdoors"

Shortly after we returned from our Gettysburg trip, we headed out as a family of four. We packed up bikes, a few toys, and enough easy meals and snacks for a weekend. Then the four of us and ten-year-old Sierra piled into the truck and headed less than an hour away to Chain O' Lakes State Park.

Within hours of our arrival, Lydia and Ethan were riding their bikes, digging in the dirt, and begging to go to the swings across from our campsite. Our camping dog, who had spent many trips with us digging in the dirt herself, stretched her aching joints and settled back into camping life for the first time in four years.

Soon we were headed out on the chain of lakes from which the state park derives its name. Our rented canoe maneuvered through the narrow, foliage-lined waterways connecting one small open body of water to the next. Because the kids were too young to help with the rowing or steering, they sat in the middle of the canoe mesmerized by the algae and plant life growing in the waterways. This was not something they would see while playing in our yard, driving around the streets and highways in and around Fort Wayne, or even visiting the children's zoo. We had opened up a whole new world to them, their smiles a reward for my aching, ill-prepared rowing muscles.

For thirty-six hours they had their undistracted parents all to themselves. We couldn't turn on a TV to entertain them. I wasn't running around doing laundry. Neither of their parents could get onto their computers and become engrossed in work or social media.

And we discovered it was the perfect time to start teaching them how to help with age-appropriate tasks. Most Indiana state parks don't have water available at the campsite. So both kids helped Jeff as he poured water from the jugs into our water tank in the camper. Then they helped me shuck corn for dinner. Instead of feeling like a chore, our outdoor setting added a sense of adventure to the monotonous tasks. They enjoyed helping at the campsite.

For the remainder of the summer, we kept returning to the outdoors whenever the opportunity presented itself.

Our second weekend trip was to one of Jeff's favorite childhood haunts. Throughout his childhood, Jeff's family traveled to Pokagon State Park in Angola, Indiana. They went camping there during the summer and fall months and returned in the winter months to do the toboggan run on the park's refrigerated track. I was supposed to initially visit Pokagon with Jeff and his family during our first married Christmas. Jeff had convinced his parents and siblings to reserve rooms in the state park lodge for two days of indoor pool fun, hot tub relaxation, and trips up and down the steep toboggan run hill.

Unfortunately, that first married Christmas was not our year.

The day we were supposed to leave, Jeff came down with a violent case of stomach flu, which hit me a few days later. A trip to the lodge would have to wait.

Now, years later, we lived less than an hour away. We found a site in Pokagon at the end of July and spent the weekend riding bikes and playing on the multiple camp playgrounds.

Now, truly for the first time ever, we were presenting our kids with hands-on learning experiences. They walked around the Pokagon

Nature Center looking at the taxidermy stuffed animals, asking questions about the park wildlife, ordering us to read signs, and petting the turtle creeping around one of the displays. It became an expected part of family camping trips, no matter how old they got.

Sure, we stayed at a campsite without a truly flat surface for our camper. Yes, we were still inexperienced at parking and setting up camp with an extra vehicle. And we inadvertently gouged out a portion of the grass and bent the stab jacks while trying to get into our uneven and sloped site. But we weren't looking back. I wasn't ready for the summer to end and with it the opportunity to continue camping nearly every weekend as a family.[1]

Near the end of the summer, we took the hybrid up to Michigan for a trip to Warren Dunes. Visiting Lake Michigan was nothing new for our kids, but we hadn't yet camped near the lake with them. Now that we had dived back into camping, we looked forward to the opportunity to take our kids to The Mitten with the freedom to stay in our own quarters instead of choosing which parents were going to house us.[2]

We left shortly after Jeff got off work on a Friday afternoon. But between the time change and a stop for dinner, it was dusk by the

---

1. We recently returned to Pokagon for a weekend camping trip and drove around the different campground loops in an attempt to find the site that caused us so much trouble as novice RV campers. I was embarrassed to discover that none of the potential candidates looked nearly as difficult as we had built it up in our heads.

2. Our parents live less than half a mile from each other. It's not as convenient as it sounds.

time we arrived at the state park. As soon as parking the camper got difficult, I got so flustered that I was useless as a partner. I became completely unsure of what Jeff wanted from me and incapable of clearly communicating what he needed to do. So we ended up blocking traffic for what seemed forever. Jeff's parents arrived during the chaos, only adding to our own tension, as they wanted to both see their grandchildren and try to help us out of our mess. The growing number of people trying to direct Jeff through the darkness into our tree-lined site just added to my frustration. I felt useless to my husband, and Jeff was disgruntled at no one present being any kind of real help. The drop off between the road and the site was enough that our little Roo, with very little clearance between the frame and the ground, scraped along the gravel drive as Jeff finally backed into our spot.

Tired and on the verge of fighting in front of Jeff's parents, our kids, and the entire campground, we got to the business of setting up camp while the kids excitedly piled out to see their grandparents. Slowly but surely, we settled into our camping weekend at the lake.

On Saturday we took the kids to the playground to swing and climb and run around. We invited friends and family over for outdoor cooking and fellowship around the fire ring. On Sunday, we unsuccessfully attempted the climb to the top of the sand dunes before dipping our feet in the lake. Both kids struggled with the sand constantly shifting underneath them, their feet sliding back a couple of inches with each step they took, no matter how large a step they attempted. By the end of the weekend, we had experienced all that lake life had to offer and returned home sun-soaked and content.

Even after another weekend in Michigan for my cousin's wedding and an impulsive weekend at Ouabache State Park in Bluffton, Indiana, Jeff wasn't done camping for the year. He was determined to have the ultimate fall camping trip to mirror the fall weekends he celebrated in Pokagon during childhood. He finally discovered Brown County State Park—the same state park where Sierra had disrupted an entire band of horse riders—had a full-fledged fall festival, in-cluding trick-or-treating through the campground.

It didn't take much to convince me. After years of feeling trapped by our move to Fort Wayne, I discovered we didn't have to stay put all of the time. In the fall I returned to a teaching job I loved. When the loneliness of life in a city where we had few contacts outside of work hit, I reminded myself of the joy I felt camping with our family of four plus a dog. In the end, Jeff and I didn't care if it would be a three- to four-hour drive, or that we would have to set up in the dark, or that we were risking camping in freezing temperatures. We were sold.

For that first family trip to Brown County, we got one of the last available campsites. We arrived at Brown County State Park around seven o'clock on a Friday night. The sun was already down, the tem-peratures were quickly dropping, and we still needed to eat dinner. Ethan and Lydia busied themselves by settling into the piles of dried leaves on our campsite. I groaned when I realized our daughter was still donning the tulle skirt she'd worn to school that day. She refused to change into warmer clothes if that meant taking off her frilly attire. But once her fingers started to get cold, she welcomed the heat inside the camper and finally relented to a weekend of wearing a coat and pants.

While the weekend was surprisingly devoid of rain or ice, it was still cold. But it wasn't enough to keep us from exploring everything the state park had to offer families. The last time we had been in the park we had been a young married couple, childless and uninterest-ed in the nature center and the playgrounds. Now we watched our children digging in the dirt, creating natural artwork with leaves and sticks, climbing on slides, swinging on the swings, and learning from the rangers eager to answer questions from curious little kids.

When it was time for the official festivities, we gawked at the incredible displays around the two main loops. Orange and purple lights, fake cobwebs stretching across tree branches, inflatables of every size and kind set up around campers and tents, and adults without small children dressed up in costumes—the entire state park came alive with spooky scenes and goofy ghoulishness. Jeff and I didn't have to discuss it. We knew we would return.

That Saturday evening, bundled up in coats, hats, and mittens, our little Rapunzel and pirate took their candy buckets around the nature center trail and then from campsite to campsite to collect more candy than they had ever gathered trick-or-treating in our neighborhood. Jeff and I returned home with a pile of positive parenting memories. Our aging and admittedly ornery dog had enjoyed the attention of family and the chance to lay outside, undisturbed. It had been the perfect end to a four-month camping marathon.

In four months, we had taken our kids to three different Indiana state parks and one Michigan state park. We had hiked, canoed, and biked, being more physically active as a family than we had ever been before. We potty trained two-year-old Ethan by having him take frequent potty breaks in the trees lining our various campsites. And Jeff got to relive his childhood through our children's eyes.

For me, camping helped me feel less trapped by a town that still didn't feel like home. The chance to get away for weekends distracted me from the long list of projects I kept devising for a house I both loved and loathed.

But more than anything, Jeff and I connected in a way we hadn't for years. The outdoors, after all, were what had brought us together in the first place.

Chapter 14
Another New Camper, New Possibilities

WHEN WE BOUGHT THE Roo, there were so many things we didn't know. We didn't know if it would actually make camping more possible. We didn't know how much camping we would do with it. We didn't know anything about pulling a camper and driving long distances with an extra 25 to 30 feet behind us.

In short, we basically knew nothing.

But once we had our camper safely stored in our oversized driveway for the winter and were able to talk and evaluate the four months of camping we had done as a family, Jeff and I knew a lot more. Soon Jeff was already talking about the next camper and what it would need to include to justify buying something bigger.

We realized we wouldn't be able to keep our son and daughter sharing a double bed forever. Jeff pointed out our desire for longer trips, and I realized we wanted more interior room for those times when we would be gone for longer than a few days. Plus, Jeff and I wanted a little more privacy and separation from our kids.

We had also just finished paying off our car, and our credit card debt was disappearing every month. We were in a much better financial position than we had been even a year earlier before we discussed buying *any* kind of camper.

At the end of that winter, we returned to the Fort Wayne RV Show and fell in love with a bunkhouse camper we could afford. It had everything we had listed on our "must-have" list. There were bunk beds in the back with storage so the kids could pack their clothes, books, and toys in their own cabinets. There was a full outdoor kitchen with a dorm-sized refrigerator and two-burner stove so I could cook outside without setting up extra equipment. It had sliding doors to the main bedroom so we could shut out the kids. And there was enough floor space for Sierra to find her own spot without worrying about the humans disrupting her personal space.

So we did it. We bought the camper we really wanted. And we couldn't wait to get out on the road again.

Our test run with the new camper was a return to Chain O'Lakes State Park. It was a location close enough that we didn't have to drive very far and could still return home if we discovered we needed something else. It gave us a chance to try out everything our camper had to offer while also celebrating Lydia's fifth birthday.

Our next summer of camping had begun. We headed up to Pokagon State Park for Memorial Day weekend, enjoying a weekend with my youngest sister, Johanna, and one of her best friends. We filled the weekend with short hikes, playground climbing and swinging, and putting our feet in the lake. Then we drove back to southern Indiana. After years away from our Indianapolis church's yearly campout, we decided to once again join the fun. It felt good to kill two birds with one stone, going on a camping trip and celebrating our son's third birthday the same weekend.

While most of the camping crew had changed from our years living in Indy, the most important part of the trip was camping with my sister Rachel's family. It gave the cousins much-needed time to play together and reacquaint themselves with family they didn't see nearly enough. We loved the moments we got to escape as a family of four, but from time to time it was nice to also share that camping experience with close friends and family.

Soon it was 2 AM, and I was still talking to my sister in the bathroom. Ethan, in the wee hours of his birthday, rolled out of his bed, falling from the top bunk and hitting his head on the ladder leading up to Lydia's bunk.

As soon as Jeff heard him fall on the floor and discovered Ethan's head wound, he raced to the closest camp bathroom in hopes he would find me there. Then he banged on the door and yelled, "Sarah, your son fell out of bed, and he's bleeding!"

The gossip session with my little sister stopped in an instant as panic settled in. My son was hurt and I hadn't been there to immediately comfort and fix him. I raced across the dark campground and miraculously jumped over the shadows of tree roots without falling flat on my face. Rachel headed in the opposite direction to get one of her best friends, who also happened to be a nurse.

Minutes later, I was holding my son in my lap. Ice and a washcloth were pressed against the back of his head, while our resident nurse did her best to assess a tired, sad little boy. In the end, we decided to stay put. The closest emergency room was almost an hour away. We would have access to a nurse for at least the next twelve hours, and he was scheduled for his yearly doctor check-up within the next week. We watched him for signs of a concussion through the rest of the night, but by morning he was ready to play with his cousins again.

Ethan started his third birthday with a bang, and we bought a rail guard before our next camping trip to keep that from happening again.[1]

We got back on the road for the Fourth of July, traveling to Potato Creek State Park near South Bend, Indiana. It was close enough to our parents in Michigan that if we wanted to, we could also take a day trip for some time at the lake as well. So we spent a day exploring the park and its nature center. Then the next day ended with a perfect Lake Michigan fireworks display on the Fourth of July.

---

1. He will have a scar on the back of his head to remember that trip for the rest of his life. The shorter his hair, the more obvious the scar.

On our last night in the park, Jeff took the kids to a ranger-led presentation on bats and learned about the different ways bats help the ecosystem.[2] The kids excitedly ran up to me later with plans for a bat house in our backyard.

Next was Ouabache State Park, this time with the family of one of Jeff's friends from work. Our kids relished the attention of older pre-teen twin girls, while we enjoyed campfires and hiking with another couple who shared our love for camping. Even though it was unusually cold for July, we climbed the fire tower, visited the bison preserve, and swam in the state park pool. Our kids stretched their legs on the playground in our camping loop. We occasionally checked on them to make sure they were playing nicely with other kids while letting them have just the littlest bit of independence.

The additional amenities of our new Gray Wolf made it possible to also use it for lodging when we weren't exclusively camping. When my baby sister Johanna announced she was getting married at the church camp where she and my brother-in-law met, everyone started scrambling to figure out where they were going to stay. There were cabins around the campground available for family members, but if we were going to a camp, we wanted to be able to take our camper. Thankfully, the camp also had spots for tents and RVs, so we made our reservation and took our camper for an outdoor destination wedding.

It was a perfect August weekend in Michigan, surprisingly pleasant with low humidity and cool nights. The day after the wedding we served as home base for my other sisters, brothers-in-law, and nieces and nephews. I made Sunday morning breakfast at our camper and then sent the kids down to the lake for some quality bonding time before we all had to head home.

And the camping wedding worked! Lydia, who was the flower girl, still managed to get clean and presentable by the time we had to have her ready for pictures. Ethan and his boy cousins got to play in

---

2. I missed it because I went back to get bug spray and the group left without me.

a considerable amount of dirt. And because we were camping where the wedding and reception were all taking place, we were able to put the kids into bed at a relatively decent hour and still have adult time once my sister and her new husband had left for the night.

With the end of summer came the anticipation for our final fall weekend away. We once again decided to celebrate Halloween by making the three-hour trek to southern Indiana. We hiked on nature trails through forests of red and orange and gold. We shed sweatshirts and jackets as the unseasonably warm temperatures climbed to 80 degrees, and we wondered why we hadn't brought shorts for our end-of-October camping trip.

This time we were determined to be in the thick of the weekend activity. That night we put out an unsupervised bowl of candy so we could contribute to the campground trick-or-treating festivities. Then we took our little Ariel and Darth Vader around to fill up their own buckets. Our second round of Halloween camping was a huge success, and we settled in for a cold winter as we dreamed of where we wanted to go once the snow melted away.

Chapter 15
Do You Know About Floyd Collins?

WHEN JEFF AND I moved to Indianapolis in 2005, it was a fresh start for our careers and our marriage. Finding new opportunities for camping was a part of that imperfect transition as a couple. But during certain seasons, embracing those new opportunities was easier said than done.

Shortly after we moved to Indianapolis, my principal asked me to direct the spring musical in addition to the fall play. As a result, Jeff and I didn't make any plans for spring break because I had absolutely no idea what kind of work I would need to do during that week away from school. When I discovered my technical director wanted to put set building for my spring production of *Cinderella* on hold during spring break, Jeff and I decided we didn't want to simply stay at home. So we looked for something we could do that would be quick, relatively cheap, and new.

That's how we ended up at Mammoth Cave National Park.

Mammoth Cave had been on our radar since planning our honeymoon to Tennessee several years earlier. We were looking for cheap and adventurous places to explore while we were in the Smoky Mountains and one of the tourist options that came up was Mammoth Cave. But when we learned it was nowhere near the Smoky Mountains, we abandoned the idea of Mammoth Cave altogether.

Years later, our home in central Indiana was less than a three-hour drive from Kentucky. The pictures of the region looked beautiful, and Jeff and I were ready to do some cave exploring. So we packed up Sierra and our camping gear, then headed south. We made reservations at the national park lodge for our first night and paid for Sierra to spend the night in the kennel directly across from the lodge.

We pitched our tent the next day in the national park campground and set out to explore. Mammoth Cave National Park encompasses the world's longest-known cave system, with a total of 400 explored miles.[1] During the two full days we were there, we took two different tours and planned for the next time we came to visit. And we did return the following year, for a nearly identical getaway. Honestly, it forced me to take a mini-vacation while I was in the yearly midst of production for the spring musical, something Jeff knew I needed. And he needed me to take time to focus on *us* before the busy end of the school year.

It was at Mammoth Cave that I finally gave in to Jeff's suggestion of a national parks passport book. We paged through it together, dreaming about future vacations across the country.

Then we had Lydia.

And we moved.

Three years later, when Jeff finally got me back outdoors, Mammoth Cave returned our destination dream list.

The fact that we returned to Mammoth Cave National Park twice in our childless years was a pretty clear indicator we had a deep appreciation for both the national park and the surrounding area.[2] It was time to share one of our favorite places with our kids.

---

1. "Mammoth Cave National Park (U.S. National Park Service)." *National Parks Service*, U.S. Department of the Interior, 22 May 2018, www.nps.gov/maca/index.htm.

2. That second trip to Mammoth Cave as a family took place during our less-than-ideal family vacation to the southeast United States less than a month before our move back to Indiana. But that has become a story for another book.

It had been a miserably cold winter, following a miserably snowy winter the year before. Jeff and I hoped the venture into Kentucky would give us a break from the severe northern cold that still lingered into late March. But we woke up on our first morning at a KOA only to discover a frozen water hose and a stream of water coming from the water spigot of the campsite across from us. Immediately, Jeff checked to ensure the freeze had not damaged any of our own equipment. And I began to dress everyone in layers to prepare for changing temperatures throughout the day.

The frigid air slowly warmed throughout the morning, and we made our first stop at the sign leading into the park so we could commemorate Lydia and Ethan's first trip to Mammoth Cave with a picture. We then hiked down the short trail to Sand Cave—part of the elaborate cave network in the region but still set apart from the main national park. As had become tradition, we read the signs out loud to our kids as we went.

It had been years since Jeff and I had been to the park, so there was a lot about the park trails we didn't remember. Our three and five-year-old were curious creatures depending on us to fill in the knowledge gaps when pictures weren't enough. The kids wanted to know what was so important about this small cave in the ground. So I turned to the nearest sign and started reading the long story about Floyd Collins. He was an entrepreneur who spelunked his way into Sand Cave before his foot dislodged a twenty-seven-pound rock that landed on his ankle, trapping him in the cave.[3] I had already informed my children about Floyd Collins' death in the cave nearly 90 years ago before I completely registered what I was reading to them.

Three-year-old Ethan loved the story. He spent the next two days asking every park ranger who would stop to listen if they would com-

---

3. "'I'm Trapped, and Trapped for Life!'." *National Parks Service*, U.S. Department of the Interior, 23 May 2018, www.nps.gov/maca/learn/historyculture/trapped.ht m.

ment on the fate of Floyd Collins. Most of the park rangers, trained to talk about the cave system and not the history of a man who died exploring a *different* cave, didn't know how to respond to our inquisitive little boy.

Lesson learned? Perhaps read signs for ourselves before reading them out loud.

When we finally arrived at Mammoth Cave proper, we took the kids on the Historic Tour, a two-mile walk through the traditional historic spots of the main cave. Our daughter made friends with another little girl on the tour, and we had to keep our eyes and ears open so we didn't lose her to an unexplored passage in one of the largest cave systems in the world. The two-mile hike through the cave explored multiple formations, a huge, naturally created open room near the entrance of the cave, passages both narrow and wide, and the spot where one particularly creative minister led his congregation for weekly Sunday services. Both kids' eyes remained wide through the whole tour, taking in every detail of the underground wonderland.

The next day we took the Domes and Dripstones Tour in another section of the park away from the visitor's center. The tour required a bus ride and took us on 500 narrow, steep stairs before a series of passageways passing domes and pits demonstrating the awesome formations throughout the cave system. By the end, it was a lot of climbing for our three- and five-year-olds, and they welcomed a picnic lunch in the sunshine once we were back on the surface.

We took a break from cave exploration and headed to Abraham Lincoln's birthplace for another National Parks passport stamp. Both Lydia and Ethan had received their own passport books on a previous trip to the Smoky Mountains and they had already learned the excitement of filling up their own books with new places and experiences. Or at least, they fed off of their mom's excitement.

We arrived at Lincoln's Birthplace an hour before it closed to the public. Earlier in the day, we had helped our preschooler and kindergartener complete their own Junior Ranger books at Mammoth.[4] Still, we hesitated to get copies of new Junior Ranger booklets with limited time to complete them. We picked them up anyway, viewed the memorial with a replica of Abraham Lincoln's cabin when he was a little boy, and stretched our legs around the grounds.

The kids finished their Junior Ranger tasks just in time to get sworn in as Junior Rangers for the second time that day, and then we headed back to our campsite. We wrapped up our trip to Mammoth enjoying the activities at the campground. I made dinner. Jeff, whose grandfather had taught him to love fishing when he had been as young as our children, broke out some fishing poles and took the kids fishing at the campground's fishing pond.

The kids were thrilled to spend time learning something new from their dad. I, on the other hand, had no desire to join in the fun. I have never seen the allure of fishing. I don't understand any of it: the worms are gross, sitting and waiting for fish to bite makes me antsy, and I have no desire to touch a live fish, let alone prepare it for food. After years of me turning my nose at sitting on a dock, our kids had suddenly given Jeff something I never could: fishing companionship.

Instead, I walked our new puppy Bella around the campground as many times as she would let me while the rest of the family fished, and we lit the perfect s'more-making campfire. Jeff and I enjoyed peacefully staring into the dying embers after both kids crashed into bed, thankful for a nearly perfect trip to one of our favorite places.

We headed home just in time, facing rain and high winds as we traveled back toward Fort Wayne. Jeff gripped the steering wheel with white knuckles and I repeatedly asked the kids to sit quietly while we worked through the nasty weather and the beginning of

---

4. The National Parks Junior Ranger program encourages children of all ages to learn more about the parks while they are visiting. The activities are age appropriate and, combined with their passports, we hoped to help our kids build a collection of Junior Ranger badges. It added a new element to our national parks experiences and became a cool collector item from each national park we visited for as long as the kids were willing to do them.

spring construction in southern Indiana. In many ways, we were still traveling rookies, and this was the longest trip we had ever attempted with our kids while hauling our camper. I'd become used to Jeff being the less reactive parent, and watching him nervously captain our truck sent my normally low blood pressure through the roof. Suddenly the rest and relaxation we'd achieved from our time away was out the window.

As we approached our old exit in Indianapolis, we noticed smoke coming from the left side of our camper. We pulled off at the exit to investigate, only to discover that a piece of the brake had come loose while we were bouncing around the construction zones earlier in our trip. It appeared that the tire would get us home, but the tension inside the truck increased even more as we slowly made our way through the last 120 miles of our trip.

Despite the traveling issues on our way home, it was still the perfect quick spring break trip. Both kids returned with a new love for caves. Lydia had gotten to explore underground palaces, and Ethan excitedly tried to explain the fate of Floyd Collins to his preschool teacher (prompting her to ask us later what exactly he was talking about).

Jeff and I still hold on tenderly to the memories of that trip. It's one I hope we never forget.

Chapter 16
Lives in Transition

I DIDN'T WANT TO stay in Fort Wayne.

More honestly, I never wanted to live in Fort Wayne in the first place and I never learned to accept it.

And after five years of Jeff's best attempts to help me settle in, I still didn't feel like Fort Wayne was home.

I know that one of the many reasons Jeff pushed so hard to buy the first camper was to make life in Fort Wayne more bearable. He hoped it would ease the waves of depression and loneliness that had plagued me since we left Indianapolis. And it did help. But while I loved my job and was proud of my newly earned master's degree, I still felt trapped in a city where I had few friends and didn't feel like I belonged. I was also plagued with guilt as I watched Jeff thrive in his new role, moving from a production scheduling job to being the head of IT. He had become a valuable member of a team that wouldn't easily let him go.

Then, during the winter of 2013-2014, Fort Wayne got nearly sixty inches of snow, more than 30 inches above average for a single winter. I didn't attend school for a full week six weeks in a row. The following winter didn't deliver nearly as much snow, but it was so cold. For the first time since moving into our house, we had to run space heaters in our laundry room to keep the pipes from freezing.

After those two winters in a row, Jeff was finally ready to discuss leaving the American Midwest, which he had called home his entire life. We were both ready to leave the state that had been our home for 13 years.

Maybe part of me was restless because I had lived in the same region for so long after a childhood of cross-country moves. Maybe I was still wishing we had experienced a little more adventure right after we got married instead of immediately settling into Indiana. Maybe I was just tired of snow and bone-chilling cold every winter.

Moving also meant transplanting my two small children and completely upending their lives. I had grown up in a family where geographical disruptions were just a fact of life, and I had determined I wasn't going to do that to my kids. Now, it appeared history was repeating itself. If we were going to do this, we needed to do it before both of our kids were in school full-time. It needed to be a leap worth taking, something none of us would regret.

With Jeff's career shift into IT, it seemed like it would be fairly easy for him to get a job anywhere, but it wasn't guaranteed because it would depend on the industry needs wherever we moved. However, if I wanted to stay in Lutheran education and continue to teach at Lutheran high schools, my southern options were limited. It was my desire to not move to public education that narrowed down where we could look for new jobs.[1] This was especially true if I wanted to make a lateral move that wouldn't put me in a smaller school with more responsibility than I already had.[2]

I searched for open options, and it appeared Texas had the best possibilities for a job.

"I don't want to raise Texans," Jeff said at my discovery.

---

1. I would also face the challenge of licensing in a new state. While I would maintain my Indiana license, a move to public education would mean immediately working to get relicensed in a new state, which would complicate the application process.

2. My years of teaching in Chicago and Indianapolis taught me I didn't want to return to that level of responsibility. I was now the mom of two growing kids. I preferred to spend my after-school hours with them, not doing hours of extracurriculars.

"Does Nevada sound better?" I asked, knowing the answer. I always thought it would be fun to visit, but Vegas didn't fit either of our personalities.

He sighed. "Okay, I guess put your name on the list for the Texas district. We'll see what happens."

So when a position opened up at a high school in north Houston, it felt right. It took a long time for all of the details to work out, but eventually, Jeff's apprehensions about raising Texans subsided when he made another observation.

"Hey," Jeff said with an impish grin, "this means we can camp year-round now."

So many elements of our lives were in transition.

We said goodbye to Sierra early in 2015. She had been six years old when we finally brought Lydia home from the hospital. Like many parents who bring their human babies home to meet the furry members of their family, we had dreams of Sierra welcoming a human sister with open paws.

She did not.

She never got over being "replaced" by the crying human with white-blond hair. Shortly before Ethan was born, she blew out her right hind knee and suffered a slow recovery. And despite her puppy-like rebound when our family started camping again, her eyes, ears, and joints showed signs of her age.

During the bitterly cold winter of 2015, we made the difficult decision to put Sierra to sleep. Jeff and I sobbed as we sat on the floor next to our first baby and watched the breath leave her body. We returned to both of our kids sitting in the exam room with one of the vet techs. They saw the paw print, collar, and no Sierra, and they suddenly understood our dog wasn't coming home.

I grieved the loss of my first pet. I was wracked by the guilt of not being as good of a caretaker as I should have been in her later years. I couldn't stop thinking of all of the ways we could have done better by her as we expanded our family. A house with four humans suddenly felt so empty, yet I wasn't ready to consider the responsibility of bringing a new pet into our home.

But Jeff started searching online for shelters within hours of leaving the vet.

A few days later, Jeff handed me his laptop. A picture of a red and gold fluffy puppy stared at me from the screen. "Look, Sarah. She's named Fuzzy Wuzzy. How could you possibly say no?"

I started emphatically shaking my head. "Jeff, we just put Sierra to sleep. Don't you think we need to give it more time? How would a new dog fit into our family?"

"The house is empty, Sarah." My husband, who had always had a dog growing up, struggled with a petless house for the first time in nearly twelve years. "It needs a dog. *We* need a dog. And how could you say no to that face?"

It turns out—I couldn't. The moment we met her caretaker and I picked her up, I didn't want to put Fuzzy Wuzzy down.

Before we brought her home, we had already determined we were going to go from a one-dog household to a two-dog family. We never stopped believing that one of our mistakes was never getting Sierra a canine companion. This time we would do better. We promised both kids that once our new dog had adjusted to our family, we would start looking for another dog to complete the Styf pack.

Lydia rechristened the puppy Bella, after Clarabelle's dog on *Mickey Mouse Clubhouse*. I inwardly cringed as I emphatically announced on Facebook and to my students that our new puppy's namesake came from a cartoon, not *Twilight*. And we assured Ethan he would get to name the next puppy.

When we decided to move to Texas, the painful loss from five months earlier seemed to fit. Sierra never would have been able to handle living in Texas. But Bella, who had only known part of one Midwest winter, was able to quickly adjust to a hotter climate.

Six months later, when we brought home a yellow lab mix named JT, our house and hearts were full.

It was a season of so much ending—and so many new beginnings.

Chapter 17

"Nothing Beats the Shores of Lake Michigan"

Our love story started on Lake Michigan when Jeff took me to the fireworks at St. Joseph, Michigan's Silver Beach for our first date. It was the Fourth of July, one month after our high school graduation and a mere three weeks after mutual friends introduced us to each other. After getting separated during the actual fireworks display and spending the entire show in different locations in the parking lot, we walked up and down the beach together for hours. The soft, cold sand squished between our toes as we waited for the endless line of cars to finally clear out so Jeff could take me home.

No matter how far we moved away from home, a trip to our parents was never complete without at least a drive past the lake. I spent much of my childhood proud of the fact that I was born in Southern California, trying to wear my native birth and first year of life like a badge. But I wasn't raised on the Pacific Coast; I was a Michigander. My first memories of water were toes in the water of Lake Huron when visiting my grandparents in Ontario or my parents driving us to Lake St. Clair during unbearable summer heat waves. As much as I may appreciate a beautiful ocean sunset photograph, I don't appreciate salt water nearly as much as fresh water.[1]

---

1. It's a fact that drove Jeff crazy when we went to Hawaii to celebrate our 20th wedding anniversary. He wanted to spend more time at the beach. I wanted to visit all the national park sites, instead.

But of all the lakes I have visited, my love for Lake Michigan only continues to grow over the years. And the lake has played a role throughout our camping history, beginning with that very first camping dry run when we needed to try out our fresh equipment as a newly married couple. Warren Dunes State Park served as our host for our tent's virgin camping trip.

From the moment we met, Jeff shared stories of camping as a child. My childhood memories involve visiting family all over the country and Canada, staying in the houses of strangers, and random sightseeing stops between those visits. But his childhood consisted of weeks and weekends visiting state parks in Michigan and Indiana, the games he and his family played to ward off rain-related boredom—and of course, camping.

A couple of those state parks from Jeff's youth were right along the shores of Lake Michigan, including Grand Haven State Park in Michigan. We managed to reserve a spot in that park once, well before we had children. Our campsite was right on the beach, and the first night we were there we were awakened by a quick thunderstorm coming up off the lake. We had never experienced water in our tent before, but the rain came down so hard and fast we didn't know what hit us. We stayed in bed, convinced we would wake up to wet sand surrounding the tent and nothing else. But when we got up to open the tent flap the next morning, our feet landed in puddles of water and wet sand *inside the tent*. We managed to dry out the tent interior and continued camping through the weekend. I reveled in walking along the boardwalk hand-in-hand with my husband, riding our bikes, and getting ice cream along the way.

Jeff was particularly excited to relive his childhood with a visit to the Grand Haven Musical Fountain. He had spent years telling me about all the times his family had visited the spot to witness the lights and water jets choreographed to a different musical number every night.

"You don't understand, honey. It's so cool!" he raved on our drive there.

Unfortunately, sometimes our memories are better than reality.

The only night we had available was Sunday, and we were in Dutch Christian Reformed territory. It became clear very quickly that the water show was worship-related, choreographed to sacred church music. Slow, somber, classic hymns accompanied the halfhearted lights and water show to match.

I tried to help Jeff laugh it off as we walked away. "I guess we just showed up on the wrong night."

He swallowed his disappointment in stride, and we haven't been back since.

Our children's earliest memories of water were of trips up to Lake Michigan when we visited both sets of grandparents.

As babies, they jumped the waves in Jeff's arms.

As soon as they could sit and dig, they learned to build mounds and trenches using wet sand, watching the waves fill the holes they created right on the shore.

They climbed partial dunes during our first Lake Michigan camping trip and walked with us along the St. Joseph pier at sunset.

Because the lake had been so important to us, we made sure it was important to our children as well.

Months before Jeff and I decided to move our family to Texas, we made reservations at Indiana Dunes State Park for a Fourth of July weekend with Jeff's family. At the time, we didn't know this would be our farewell camping trip to Lake Michigan.

Indiana Dunes State Park includes a beach, beach camping, and a campground that borders right on the national park. Because the park is so popular, I had to book our July reservations six months in advance. The first time we stayed in the state park we weren't able to get a spot until August, *after* school had started. So when Jeff's family decided to all camp together for the most popular beach weekend of the year, we rushed the rest of the family to reserve as soon as the online window opened, to ensure we all had campsites close to each other.

It was the perfect get-together for the Styf family. His younger sister Kara wanted to show her Florida-born-and-bred children what Michigan looked like in the summer. His older sister Kristen appreciated leaving the mountains for some quality Lake Michigan time. It was a quick trip down from southwest Michigan for Jeff's parents and youngest sister Jenni. We could camp as a family and still be close enough to watch the Fourth of July fireworks at our favorite spot: Silver Beach in St. Joseph, Michigan.

Our July return to Indiana Dunes started during an unseasonably cool holiday weekend. We bundled up in sweatshirts to watch the fireworks on the park beach, forcing Lydia to put leggings on underneath her typically skirted camping outfit. We watched as both of our kids ignored the cold and played in the sand, getting closer and closer to the shoreline and finally returning to us with wet sand-covered sleeves. Lydia loved burying her lower body in the soft, damp sand, and both kids snuggled close as the fireworks show began.

We enjoyed time as a family of four and an extended family of fourteen. Jeff's youngest sister and sister-in-law joined our foursome on the Three-Dune Challenge, a one-and-a-half-mile hike with a 552-foot vertical incline to the top of the tallest dunes in the park.

We all eventually ditched our shoes and completed the hike barefoot, each holding a kid's hand to help them step over roots and prevent a head-over-heels tumble down the other side of each dune. Bella, full of puppy energy, pulled Jeff up the hills when he wasn't holding a kid's hand. This hike offered more than a solid morning of exercise. The top of each dune revealed a breathtaking view of clear blue skies and the sun sparkling on the surface of Lake Michigan.

The nights were cold during our holiday trip, but the days were perfect. We visited the nature center where the kids played on a child-friendly shipwreck display and learned about the animals on the dunes. Lydia colored and drew inside the camper with her cousin who is only three days younger than her. We threw our sweatshirts back on to walk along the beach and capture hazy sunsets, squinting to see the Chicago skyline in the distance. We visited the national park's visitor center and stamped our passports, slowly building a collection that at the time only included locations in Indiana, Kentucky, and Tennessee.

When we'd made reservations for Indiana Dunes six months before, we'd had no idea we would be in the middle of move preparations during our weekend trip to the lake. And while we were excited about a new adventure and a much-needed fresh start over 1,000 miles away, leaving Lake Michigan was one of the more difficult parts of our move. Over the next six years, nothing beat the shores of Lake Michigan.

I had no idea how much I would miss it once we were settled in Texas.

Chapter 18
"We Are Living in a Tiny House"

"I WANT TO LIVE in a tiny house."

We had just turned off the television after watching yet another HGTV episode on tiny house living, and Lydia was enamored with the very idea of moving into an adorable little house on the property of her choice.

"Honey, we *are* living in a tiny house. We've been living in a tiny house for weeks."

"We're living in our camper, Mom. It's not the same thing."

I couldn't argue with her there.

The June before we moved to Texas we flew the whole family down to Houston to look for a house. With our Fort Wayne home already under contract, Jeff and I were optimistic we would find our dream home and move in as soon as we arrived from Indiana over a month later.

That's not exactly how it happened...

We found a house. Jeff loved it and I really liked it, but it needed some work. Our realtor suggested we offer a lot less than the asking price. When the sellers rejected our offer, we decided to hold off—and good thing we did! In late summer of 2017, that neighborhood was hit with Hurricane Harvey flooding that most certainly would have sent us out of the house for months to come. With that offer refusal, we dodged a huge bullet. But it still left us without a house to move into upon our Houston arrival.

So, Jeff took charge of the situation. "What if we just move into our camper?" he asked me one night as we weighed our options. This wasn't a new conversation, but it had always been a hypothetical, not a reality.

We needed a place to live, and we had to tow our camper down to Texas anyway. With no better options, we made reservations at an RV resort and then moved into our camper. For six weeks we lived in our 30-foot-long camper, a maximum of 300 square feet replacing the nearly 4,000 square feet we'd left behind.

The RV park we had selected wasn't a state park or even a KOA. But it had all of the amenities we could possibly want while waiting to find a new home. We did our best to cook. After years of being frustrated because his wife had no interest in fishing, Jeff broke out his old fishing poles and continued the fishing lessons that he'd started at Mammoth Cave. He and the kids fished in the lake behind our concrete slab when they needed something quiet to do without leaving the campsite. We spent time in the resort pool, grabbing free popcorn from the front office lobby. And we appreciated that we still had air-conditioning. But it didn't take us long to discover that RV living and RV camping are two completely different beasts.

In many ways, we were still RV newbies. We were weekend warriors, rarely gone for more than three days at a time. We had never taken a long road trip with the camper in tow. We never had to plan out for weeks at a time. We didn't know what it was like to spend weeks on end eating, sleeping, and living in the same small space.

And we faced plenty of challenges as a result.

Jeff held onto his job in Fort Wayne, working an IT role remotely from our camper. The kids bounced between a babysitter and then school, where Ethan continued in pre-kindergarten and Lydia started first grade. And I was learning the ropes at a new school 30 to 45 minutes away[1]. While the kids and I spent our days in climate-controlled buildings, Jeff spent every day trying to stay cool in our three-season camper not designed for days on end of temperatures over 100 de-

---

1. When we finally moved into our house, my commute got cut down to about 20 minutes in the morning, 30 minutes in the afternoon.

grees. When he could, he found refuge in the RV park business rooms. But I often returned at the end of the day to an overheated, irritable spouse who just wanted to get out of the camper. Unfortunately, after a full day of teaching, all I wanted to do was chill in my own space, but none of us had our own space.

Then there was the issue of feeding our family. We discovered the limited storage inside the RV required careful meal planning. It was a skill I had never been good at before Texas and I didn't have the time or capacity to learn right then.

Plus, it was too hot to cook. We moved to Houston at the end of July, when the heat and humidity were so oppressive most people hid in the air-conditioning until the sun went down. The last thing either of us wanted to do was cook outside and we didn't want to heat the inside of our RV. Much of the money we saved on living in the camper was spent on eating out because it was easier and cooler.

Our kids were used to camping in state parks where they had access to playgrounds and trails and the general outdoors. They missed having space where they could run, play, and climb. When we needed to get food, we frequently found ourselves at McDonald's or Chick-fil-A for the sole purpose of a cool playground where they could burn off some of their energy. Unfortunately for us, it meant fast food. But at least it got all of us out of the camper so we could stretch our legs without feeling like the walls were closing in on us.

I missed the natural movement around a traditional home and depended on longer nightly dog walks around the camper loops with our puppy Bella. Jeff would come with me, giving us a few minutes to talk away from the kids while they settled into bed. Quickly, I came to long for wooded trails that would take me out of the city and away from the concrete jungle where we found ourselves. Thank goodness for the RV park's pool. It was where Lydia learned how to swim without a life jacket and Ethan discovered how to comfortably put his head underwater.

For me, the biggest technical challenge was the camper's bathroom, which was getting a bigger workout than ever before. Since we had prioritized staying at state parks, we made it a habit to use state park bathrooms for everything: brushing teeth, washing faces and hands, showering, and especially using the toilets. We occasionally used the sink, but we never took showers because the wastewater filled up the tank in a matter of minutes. So our shower stall was usually our clothes hamper. Now, with limited storage, we crammed towels wherever they would fit and toiletries for four people spilled all over the sink as I searched for safe places to put my makeup and hair straightener, often stuffing them back into the storage in our bedroom.

With a full hook-up for six weeks, we easily gave in to our kids' needs to use the bathroom that was closest to them. Jeff and I still took showers down at the resort bathrooms, but we often washed our kids in the shower in the camper because it was more convenient, even with a small hot water tank. This led to another camping first for me: getting over my fears of helping Jeff empty the black water—sewage—tank. Unlike the movies, it wasn't messy or smelly. It involved a simple pull of a lever.

Once it became a regular part of our lives, we learned it wasn't nearly that big of a deal.

Our living space started to feel smaller with each passing week. Once school started, Lydia had homework. I had grading and lesson planning to do. And every morning after he dropped the kids off at school, Jeff spread out his work supplies on the inside table, only to put it all away once we were home and starting the dinner and bedtime routine. We were on top of each other, and our stuff was on top of our stuff. Stuffed animals and books made their way out of the kids' sleeping space. Mountains of dishes inexplicably got taller in the sink, even though we weren't home to dirty them. And the pile of mail and housing documents grew exponentially.

The reason why we'd had so many fond memories of camping up to that point was because camping usually took us away from everything that separated us from each other. But during that short season in our life, the thing that was supposed to take us away from it all was actually keeping us trapped *with* it all.

So Jeff and I tried to get creative with getting to know our new hometown. We drove around the highways of Houston, walked around too many stores, and went to too many home shows. We visited IKEA to dream about what we would be able to do once we finally had the keys to our new home.

There were days that our new house felt like the Holy Grail in Indiana Jones. I could see it. I could reach for it. I could even drive past it as many times as I wanted. But my ability to grasp it was teetering on the brink. I wanted the stability of home. I wanted our kids to have the room to run and play with their stuff in their own rooms. I wanted Bella to have the room to run around in circles without rocking the entire camper. I want to snuggle up with Jeff on the couch and watch *The Walking Dead* with our children safely asleep upstairs. I wanted to paint walls and make rooms in our new house feel like they were ours. I wanted to bring my grading pile home, spread it on a kitchen table, and just get to work. I wanted to be able to stock my pantry with food so that I could easily prepare healthy and affordable meals for my family.

Some days, it was just too much.

"I want to go back to Indianana!" Tears streamed down Ethan's face. The grief from missing everything he ever knew and frustration from weeks of living in such a tiny space were finally crashing in on our little boy.

Suddenly a full day of random tears, screaming, and generally aggressive behavior towards his sister made sense. While Jeff was out shopping with Lydia, Ethan finally burst, sobbing about how much he hated Texas. He missed his house, his bedroom (and bedroom door), and his playset. He missed his Imaginext "guys" and Captain America shield. He missed "Indianana" campgrounds that had trails and dirt and playgrounds.

He needed a return to normal—and soon.

We had found our house. We had an accepted offer. There was a pending sale sign in the front yard. We were only waiting for the final paperwork to get through. But none of that was easy to explain to our four- and six-year-olds who just wanted to have their own rooms and toys they hadn't seen in months.

We learned a lot about ourselves through our camper experiment, and I have no regrets. Now I find myself going on purging binges to get rid of every little thing that doesn't have a home—because we really can live with less.[2] And there's value in letting individual family members get alone time when we have been traveling in the camper for more than a couple of days. It took a little time, but we eventually recovered from our camper living experiment. And less than four months later, Ethan's feelings were a little less averse to our new home state.

---

2. Except paper. I will always struggle to make decisions about what papers need to go.

Chapter 19
We Just Needed to Take the Leap

I'll be honest—I wasn't immediately ready to entertain the idea of moving back in. And yet, six weeks after we moved into our house, we were poised to finally venture back outdoors for a weekend trip. Jeff and I planned to go hiking. The kids were looking forward to unrestricted biking. And we were going to enjoy some quality family time that didn't involve unpacking boxes, cleaning surfaces, painting walls, or running errands.

Then the forecast came in. Rain. Not just any, normal Midwestern rain like we were used to, but a drenching, flood-inducing rain aided by a hurricane passing over Mexico with a storm system continuing into Texas.

So our plans changed. After living in our camper for six weeks I wasn't risking floodwaters to spend a weekend *inside* our camper. Jeff initially didn't agree. He was afraid that six weeks of camper living had made me gun-shy about ever going camping again. But when he saw the ten inches of water in one of our buckets on the back patio, he conceded we had probably made the right decision. Clearly, we were still new to the consequences of Gulf Coast weather.

By the time we headed out of Houston for a weekend getaway, we were ready to move back into the camper for a weekend. Getting away meant Ethan could play with sticks as homemade lightsabers, hitting trees and fighting Darth Maul. It meant Lydia could make new friends with other girls who were also camping. It meant seeing some of the beautiful landscapes we didn't even know Texas offered.

In the 36 hours we were in Sam Houston National Forest, my family and I saw new southern plants mixed with fall leaves. We watched the beautiful sunsets over Lake Conroe. We saw our first alligator warnings (but thankfully no alligators). At night our campfire kept us warm, and during the day the sun heated the air so we didn't have to worry about hats and gloves.

Was the weekend perfect? No. Was it easy to take a weekend away from home two weeks before the end of a semester of teaching new courses in a new school? No. In fact, for the first time in a long time, I took work along with me for the weekend, spending a few hours grading AP practice essays outside at a picnic table. Did we have a series of mishaps both before leaving and on our way home? Yep. But what mattered was Jeff showing our daughter how to identify trail markers, Lydia learning how to train our new puppy JT to walk on a leash, and Ethan taking off ahead of us along a trail, asserting new-found independence. What mattered was the campfire and s'mores. What mattered was we came home better connected as a family.

I had let big changes get in the way of camping before. Jeff believed the only remedy to my hesitation was to take the leap. The longer we put it off, the more likely it was that we would never get back outdoors as a family. But Jeff said we needed to do it, and he was right. We needed to prove to ourselves we could still camp, *really* camp.

Now we were ready to explore our new state.

Chapter 20
"Back to Michigan Already?"

MOVING TO TEXAS OPENED up new opportunities for our family. After years of spending our parenting years staying close to Indiana, we started making a list of dream camping vacations. Jeff was ready to take off for Fort Wilderness and Disney World. I dreamed of heading west to Mesa Verde and Arches. Our short spring break trip to East Texas and Louisiana and a quick weekend at Goliad State Park had shown us the new possibilities in Texas.

So when I told Jeff we needed to return to Michigan during our first full summer living in Texas, he said, "We have to go back to Michigan already?"

The first summer after we moved south, my sisters and I made plans for a 40th-anniversary celebration for my parents, which meant traveling from Texas to Michigan for our summer vacation. We had two options. We could board the dogs and drive our smaller car up north and squeeze our family into spare bedrooms with everyone else also coming home with *their* families. Or we could travel up with our camper and extend our vacation for a few more days while giving us our own space to escape from family.

We chose to take our camper with us.

It was our first time prioritizing our camper as a moving hotel room. And we had so much to learn about travel beyond a weekend trip.

We left on a Friday with no plans or reservations beyond driving toward Michigan from southeast Texas. The first day consisted of nearly four hundred miles of road before we finally found a roadside

RV campground in the middle of Arkansas. The stop came with a playground for the kids and absolutely no place outside to put our dogs, but it worked for a night of sleep.

Our travel goal for the next day was Fern Clyffe State Park in Illinois. Jeff didn't stop for five hours, constantly on the lookout for a good place to temporarily park with the camper that would meet the needs of four humans and two dogs. We traveled across barren eastern Arkansas, finding nowhere to easily enter and park with an extra 30 feet hanging off our back end. Twenty miles after crossing the Missouri border, we finally pulled off at the Missouri Welcome Center where we found bathrooms, a place for Bella and JT to stretch their legs, and a playground.

I ran back and forth between the building and the truck, filling our many water bottles while Jeff held onto dog leashes and watched the kids play. Lydia had recently discovered she could successfully cross the monkey bars at any given playground. And five-year-old Ethan decided that if his seven-year-old sister could do something, so could he. Before I headed back into the rest area to fill up yet another set of water bottles, I watched our son attempt the first two monkey bars and then safely drop from a considerable height to his feet. Thankful he didn't break a leg and convinced I had nothing to worry about, I left to fill the remaining bottles.

I returned minutes later to discover my shaken husband comforting our wailing son. After I left, Ethan decided on another attempt across the bars, slipped from the first bar, landed on his feet, and then fell on his wrist. He said it hurt but nothing seemed out of place. I found as cold of an ice pack as I could, and dug around for some children's ibuprofen. Then we headed back on the road with me in the backseat trying to comfort Ethan as both kids settled in to watch *Zootopia*.

We did make it to Ferne Clyffe State Park, where we surprisingly found plenty of open campsites. We were surrounded by tall oaks and maple trees, and we enjoyed the cooler temperatures. I pointed out another playground, and our dogs were thrilled to be out of the truck.

It was a much roomier place for our whole family to settle in for the night, even if one family member was struggling with an aching arm.

The next morning we headed straight to Michigan where we spent the following week parked in Jeff's parents' yard, putting us a short walk away from my parents' house. We could walk kids and dogs back and forth between both houses to see my sisters and their kids and still return to our own space at night.

And to make our trip especially memorable, three days after Ethan's fall we discovered he had broken his arm. As Jeff's mom, a former pediatric nurse, observed her grandson, she noticed our active little boy wasn't using his left arm and encouraged us to get his arm checked. We spent part of an afternoon at urgent care getting x-rays and fighting with a Michigan doctor about our son needing a waterproof cast before we returned to hot, humid Houston. Ethan's blue-tinted cast was featured in the family photographs we took with my parents, sisters, and their families, ensuring we would never forget how that summer vacation started.

In the end, this trip helped Jeff and me learn how to plan beyond weekend camping trips. It was a skill we would both need if we were going to tackle our growing vacation bucket list.

Chapter 21
"How About We Go Camping for Thanksgiving?"

WE WERE SITTING ON the couch watching TV after the kids went to bed. Jeff looked up at me from the computer in his lap, a mischievous light in his eyes. "How about we go camping for Thanksgiving?"

I gave my husband a withering look that said everything I was thinking. *Camping in late November? Isn't it an American tradition to gather with a lot of people you may or may not like, eat too much food, and then fight shopping crowds the next day to get the very best bargains to start Christmas shopping?*

Still, I paused before responding. "I guess no one is coming down here for Thanksgiving dinner."

"Exactly!" It was then I realized he was serious.

Even during the early years of our marriage, when I was still learning how to cook basic meals, we loved hosting Thanksgiving. I didn't love the mad rush to clean our house, but Jeff and I have always enjoyed giving to others with hospitality, showing our love with an overflow of our favorite foods. We liked staying in our own home. And I honestly loved how clean our house was for about a week after we'd hosted and the trash had been carried out to the curb.

We hosted Thanksgiving for at least three of the five years we lived in Indianapolis, inviting friends who also didn't want to travel to visit family over the holidays. When we moved to Fort Wayne and my cooking skills and Jeff's grilling acumen significantly improved, we hosted at least three of those Thanksgivings. The largest event was a group of 17 people including one set of grandparents, both sets of parents, and a cousin who flew in from NYU because Indiana was closer than her home in Washington state. By our last Indiana Thanksgiving before moving to Texas, Jeff and I had mastered the art of outdoor food preparation, braving the unpredictable northern weather to grill and deep fry at least two turkeys and one ham to feed a small crowd for a couple of days of feasting and celebration.[1]

The move to Texas meant we would no longer have large crowds of family coming to our home. During our first year in Houston, Jeff's parents visited for Thanksgiving, so we gladly fixed a small dinner for six people. But our second year in Houston we had no planned visitors, so I had no legitimate reason for saying no when Jeff proposed the camping trip.

That's when I said yes.

It didn't take us long to discover we were late to the game, at least in Texas. We wanted to find a site that would be both a new and interesting location, one where we would be guaranteed nice enough weather for the end of November. State park campgrounds all around the state were already booked, which made us feel far less special about our new plans for Thanksgiving. We finally found a campground further down the Gulf of Mexico at Goose Island State Park. Since the kids and I had a full week off from school, we reserved Tuesday through Friday night. This would give us plenty of time for relaxing, exploring, and an entire day to fix our own Thanksgiving dinner at the campsite.

The first-ever Styf Campsgiving was a go.

We took off for Goose Island the Tuesday before Thanksgiving, driving two hundred miles down the coast. We arrived at dusk, which meant parking the camper in our wooded spot with only a flashlight to lead the way. By the time we all crashed into bed, Jeff and I already felt decompressed. Jeff had been traveling more for his job

---

1. We purchased a propane-powered Char-Broil oil-less deep fryer to avoid the dangers and expense of working with hot oil, and we've never regretted it.

and my schoolwork kept me busy. We had dedicated the short break to just spending time with each other outdoors. The holiday stress that normally hit us every Thanksgiving was a thing of the past. Even better, we had finally left southeast Texas, ready to explore more of the second-largest state with our trip down the coast.

Our kids woke up the next morning ready to play and explore their own little world. They were going through a serious Harry Potter phase, prompted by our family listening to the audiobooks on our summer road trip to visit family in Michigan. Our five- and seven-year-olds donned their Harry Potter robes from Halloween, carried their wands with them everywhere, and wandered all over the empty campsite next door. Lydia insisted on wearing her Ravenclaw robe for the entire day, regardless of where we traveled.

Instead of prepping from sunrise to sunset the day before Thanksgiving to host a large crowd, we spent the full day exploring our way down the coast. We walked along the pier to look out over the Gulf. We drove to the oldest coastal oak tree in Texas. The kids found other coastal oaks to climb on, stepping over the exposed roots and pulling themselves up to hang from the gnarled branches.

Then we drove toward Padre Island National Seashore. Before we left Houston, I looked up national park sites down the coast and discovered we would be within a short driving distance from the national seashore. I was determined to visit another national park before the end of the calendar year. Jeff had begrudgingly agreed.

But as we approached Corpus Christi on our way to Padre Island, Jeff saw a sign for the USS Lexington, a retired aircraft carrier anchored along the Corpus coastline and open for tours. I could see from his expression he'd already decided we had to stop. In response, I looked at the clock. It was approaching lunchtime. I had no idea how much it would cost. And I still wanted to make it to the Padre Island visitor center before it closed.

Despite all of the possible excuses hanging between us, we stopped anyway.

As we climbed the stairs from one level to the next, the kids scrambled into planes and positioned themselves behind the guns on the deck. They lay down on bunks and sat in old dentist chairs.[2] We read the signs to them and learned as a family about an aircraft carrier that had been around since World War II.

Despite my initial concerns, we still made it to the national seashore before the visitor center closed. All of us got our passport stamps and the kids got to explore the displays, the most interesting being information on the sea turtles that hatch along the beach every spring. Then we did what we had never been able to do on a Thanksgiving weekend: we walked on the beach. I smiled, capturing the moment on my phone's camera as the salty waves washed over our kids' feet and they picked up seashells along the shoreline.

We returned to the camper that night in time to have a campfire, temperatures dropping just enough to justify the long pants and sleeves to ward off the late fall mosquitoes.

The next morning we started our Thanksgiving preparations. Even though there would only be the four of us, we went all out. Jeff set up the propane-powered fryer for our turkey. I peeled potatoes and started cooking them on our three-burner stove, adding corn, gravy, and stuffing to the mix as we got closer to a cooked turkey. For a finishing touch, I used our mini pellet grill as a makeshift oven and baked Pillsbury crescent rolls.

In the end, we proved we could successfully make a traditional Thanksgiving meal entirely outside using all the equipment we already owned. The day was simple, but also oddly freeing.

Instead of spending our Thanksgiving day doing last-minute chores before everyone arrived and trying to keep the house clean after everyone finished eating, we enjoyed a peaceful, delicious meal. Instead of reading through newspaper ads to make our di-

---

2. As with all military sea vessels, the aircraft carrier was designed to meet every sailor's needs. Our military personnel also need medical care for regular ailments during peacetime as well as combat.

vide-and-conquer plans for Black Friday, Jeff relaxed in the hammock while the kids used sidewalk chalk to draw all over the concrete slab underneath our picnic table.

And when we packed up to head home on Friday, my thoughts were filled with this intimate pocket of time together as a family. The weeks ahead would be full of grading and planning and community events. But this moment, these few days in November, were just ours.

It was safe to say Campsgiving 2016 was a success.

Chapter 22
"Ready for More"

WHILE I ENJOYED THE time with family up in Michigan, our summer vacation the year after we moved to Texas never really felt like a vacation. We rushed up to Michigan, were constantly busy with family obligations, and relaxed very little. We moved south because we felt a deep need for something new and different, and we needed some space to find that as a family. After a full year in Texas, we were still struggling to figure out what that meant for our family. We had camped three times in our state in the previous year, but it felt like we were in the same rut.

The Styfs were ready for more.

That September, hungry for a weekend away, we made reservations at Lake Livingston State Park, a little over an hour from our home. The heat was still too oppressive for long morning hikes and nighttime campfires, but we did spend some time together as a family checking out the lake overviews, canoeing in the bay inlet, and taking the kids to the nature center to escape the heat. While the small trip was far from everything we wanted, Lake Livingston became one of our favorite places to go when we needed a quick weekend away.

Over the next six months, we continued to explore. Our first annual Campsgiving took our family down the coast. Jeff and I enjoyed New Orleans for our 15th wedding anniversary. We took the kids to Arkansas for spring break, enjoying the history of Hot Springs National Park, digging for diamonds at Crater of Diamonds State Park, and watching the sunset over the lake and the Ouachita Mountains in Daisy State Park.[1] Then we quickly discovered that growing kids meant different roadblocks to camping.

When both kids started soccer during our second spring in Texas, it cut into our potential spring camping time. We bought our camper with plans to bond with our kids outdoors. I knew our jobs and other family obligations would cut in on time together camping, but I never considered how our kids growing up would also affect our desire to be outdoors with them. Instead, I fell in love with watching them play sports, soaking up the sunshine while walking up and down the sidelines to cheer them on. Camping had to wait until their seasons were over and Jeff and I could reserve new state parks.

We somehow managed to plan a trip just before the arrival of Texas summer temperatures that would last us until October. On an impulse, we invited our next-door neighbors, who became quick friends within days of us moving into our house. Their son and Ethan loved and fought like brothers. Lydia willingly played with their daughter, adopting her as the little sister she would never have.[2] All of the kids entered each other's houses like they were their own. We joked about putting a gate in the fence between our two properties so they could just go back and forth without opening doors. Jeff and Mickey stayed up late during the hot summer nights, sitting outside to drink beer and talk about sports. Angela and I would talk education when we weren't lamenting the challenges of parenting.

We knew taking friends camping was a new level of friendship intimacy and we were taking a huge gamble. Mickey had fond memories of camping as a kid, but Angela had never been camping before. Her idea of a relaxing vacation involved sitting on a cruise ship, not sleeping in a tent. Still, Mickey and their kids could not wait. Jeff and

---

1. While we usually prioritized exploring our new home state, living in Southeast Texas meant we were close enough to Louisiana and Arkansas to occasionally take advantage of those state park systems as well.

2. They would have another little girl shortly after this.

I shared in the excitement but privately discussed all the things that could go wrong.

We needed this weekend to go well. Yes, we wanted our neighbors to have fun, but we also wanted to still be friends when we got home. We'd still have to live next door to each other, no matter what.

So the Styfs and the Mahals headed to Mission Tejas State Park, about two hours north of Houston. My crew got there first and set up the entire camp, including the Tent-Mahal right outside our camper. The Mahals didn't arrive until well after dark. But at that point, the only thing they still had to do was unload their clothes and bedding. The real struggle was getting excited kids into bed so the adults could enjoy some campfire time without the interruption of children.

The next day's goal was to show our friends why we found so much joy in spending an entire weekend outdoors. The dads started by taking kids to the camp office and picking up explorer packs and GPS units so we could complete the geocache challenge that someone had set up in the park ages ago.[3]

We hiked and looked for the hidden metal boxes, the kids excitedly searching for treasure all over the park. I tried to keep my fear of someone stepping on a copperhead or rattlesnake to myself. Our group crossed bridges and climbed pine-tree-lined hills. The historical replica buildings offered a glimpse of what living on the Texas frontier was like over a hundred years before. The kids climbed on playground equipment and willingly trekked on yet another trail, eager to see if they would find something better to exchange in yet another geocache box.

That night we made the mandatory camping s'mores, and our tired kids crawled into bed late but happy. Jeff and I sat up with Mick

---

3. Geocaching is an outdoor treasure hunt set up by strangers for strangers. Following an app or a GPS designed specifically for geocaching, you follow the directions to discover some kind of container with prizes for the hunters and usually a log to record names and dates. The goal is to find the treasure and leave a treasure for future adventurers, and all four kids couldn't wait to do it.

and Ang and talked under a starry night sky until both wives were falling asleep in our camping chairs. Soon, the women headed to bed long before our husbands were ready to call it a night.

The weekend had been nearly perfect, deepening our friendship beyond just being neighbors.

Our second neighbor camping trip came right in the middle of soccer season during a surprise weekend break. We headed out just over an hour outside of Houston to Huntsville State Park for a weekend of hiking, fishing, campfires, and fellowship. Our friends joined us on Saturday afternoon, which meant a morning of family hiking through the woods and the kids biking around the campsite's loop. I saw my first alligator in its natural habitat that night while the kids were fishing off the dock. The hungry gator swam back and forth beneath us, waiting for any prey to cross its path. With Huntsville as our other close getaway, it wouldn't be the last time we encountered alligators up close.

Unfortunately, our large tent finally met its end during that camping trip. After nearly 15 of years ownership, the decade of storage and disuse led to dry rot in the nylon rainfly. It started leaking in the middle of the night, and those leaks expanded until the rainfly turned into a sieve. The rain poured on our friends like it poured on my parents and sisters all those years ago in the Black Hills. Thankfully, our friends were more forgiving about the failed equipment than my sisters had been. The kids ran into our dry camper while parents packed up gear for the drive back to Houston.

After two trips, we were still friends, and we had created important memories with all of our kids in tow.

Chapter 23
Company for Campsgiving

AFTER THE SUCCESS OF our first Campsgiving, we started planning early the following spring to be more deliberate about our Thanksgiving camping. Again, we wanted a new location, but we also wanted to make sure we didn't go too far north. Plus, our numbers grew. Jeff's sister Kristen and her husband started to hint they might be interested in driving down from Colorado to join us, as long as they didn't have to drive through the whole state to get there. Our Houston friends Craig and Heather suggested they might also be interested in coming with us. So we looked for a Texas state park that would meet all of those needs. Always on the hunt for new and interesting places to camp, we initially searched for openings at Dinosaur Valley State Park near Dallas, but it was already full for the holiday.[1] Apparently, we weren't the only ones who wanted to spend Thanksgiving weekend near fossilized dinosaur tracks. So we ended up choosing another state park that was close enough for us to still allow for a day trip to Dinosaur Valley.

Cleburne State Park would be our new destination.

---

1. The state park is about an hour from Dallas. In 1937, an explorer collecting fossils discovered both sauropod and theropod tracks in the Paluxy riverbed. When the water level is low enough, like in November, park visitors can hop across the dry sections and see the tracks both underwater and on the shoreline. "Dinosaur Valley State Park." *Dinosaur Valley State Park Nature - Texas Parks & Wildlife Department*, 10 May 2024, https://tpwd.texas.gov/state-parks/dinosaur-valley/nature. Accessed 11 June 2024.

On Wednesday morning, we pulled the camper out of the storage facility and pulled in front of the house, ready to load up our standard camping supplies and then some. This wasn't just any camping trip. We were also hosting an outdoor Thanksgiving pitch-in dinner for nine additional people.

There was turkey, potatoes, gravy, crescent rolls, green beans, and all the necessary food to feed a whole crew for three days. Once again, we pulled out the oil-less deep fryer for our once-a-year turkey preparation and got it ready for cooking the turkey sitting in our RTIC cooler.

We arrived early enough at the campsite to set up our headquarters in the daylight, then we waited for Jeff's sister and family to arrive. Having traveled 200 miles north of Houston, we prepared for nights under 40 degrees. Wood was piled high and hot chocolate and coffee at the ready.

The next morning, Jeff and I dove into Thanksgiving preparations. Our friends arrived with roasted turkey and stuffing, and we were already cooking potatoes. The second turkey was in the oil-less fryer. The mini pellet grill was ready to bake the crescent rolls. And Kristen had started the collard greens. Everyone contributed, and by mid-afternoon, we had all managed to stuff ourselves with a feast spread out over a picnic table, camping tables, and the camping chairs scattered around our campsite.

The next day, instead of heading to stores to buy things we didn't need or really want, our whole crew headed to Dinosaur Valley State Park to hop across the Paluxy River, hunt for fossilized dinosaur tracks, and hike to the top of the overlook. Kids and adults carefully avoided the cool river waters. We took pictures sitting in sauropod tracks. And we sometimes hiked, sometimes climbed the long trail leading to spectacular views of the river and valley below.

When we reached the top of the overlook, we all heard the sudden dinging of adult cell phones finding service for the first time in two days. Yes, even though we were only an hour and a half from downtown Dallas, we had spent nearly 48 hours off the grid. And it had been wonderful.

Jeff and I weren't getting emails from work. No one was concerned with the latest nonsense on social media. And we had to have real conversations with each other. Decades and several cell phone upgrades later, it felt like that first camping trip I took with Jeff and Kristen the Memorial Day weekend before we got married. We laughed at each other as we all "checked in" on social media and then put our phones back away while looking across at the valley where dinosaurs had once trod.

The news of our second successful Campsgiving convinced Jeff's entire family they wanted in on the action the following year. With Kristen in Colorado, Kara and family in Florida, and Jeff's parents and youngest sister Jenni in Michigan, picking a warm enough location central enough for everyone proved to be a challenge. Jeff and I finally suggested Louisiana, proposing a state park close enough to New Orleans so we could spend a day exploring the city.

Suddenly, our quiet family Thanksgiving became decidedly less peaceful.

Kristen beat us to the campground a day early. We arrived at Tickfaw State Park after dark the following evening. With the help of a fellow camper offering their headlights and the careful placement of our LED lanterns, Jeff safely parked our camper into the spot we would establish as base camp for the next three days.

Most of the next day was spent relaxing, exploring, and waiting for the rest of the family. We welcomed Jeff's parents and two younger sisters as we prepared dinner. The sun set on a row of four tents, four cars, our camper, and five families. The firepit on our site was surrounded by 14 chairs and family members talking with each other and over each other for the first time in three and a half years.

Thanksgiving Day we all slowly woke up to sunshine and comfortable temperatures that burned off the fall chill from the previous night. A large breakfast of eggs, sausage, bacon, and everything else we could prepare satisfied the whole crew until it was time to make dinner. We filled the day with cooking, eating, and hiking around the trails in the state park, taking in the unique Louisiana vegetation and encounters with wildlife, including an alligator that appeared dormant on the banks of the park's small lake.

We spent the evening hours using our limited cell service to obsessively check the weather forecasts for the following day. The forecast was for steady rain starting at noon, and the plan was for the whole family to go to New Orleans for the day. Despite our good intentions of getting on the road early the next morning, we first had to put away chairs and tables to prepare for the possibility of rain while we were gone. Finally, we headed for the Algiers Ferry, where we would be able to park outside of the city and ride across the Mississippi River for a couple of hours of exploring in the Big Easy, echoing what Jeff and I had done two years before when we celebrated our 15th wedding anniversary.

Over the next five hours, we filled our stomachs with New Orleans cuisine, walked along historic streets, took pictures at every statue around Louis Armstrong Park, watched live street performances, ate beignets at Cafe du Monde, and finally figured out where the New Orleans Jazz National Historical Park was located.[2] And after all that concern about rain, we didn't see a drop until we were already headed back to our campsite.

The bonus for the week? The time with family. The additional bonus? When we got home we didn't have to put our house back

---

2. Unfortunately it was closed, so after two trips to New Orleans, I *still* haven't visited the national historic site.

in order from days of family revelry. It's still one of our favorite big family Thanksgivings to date.

While Jeff and I had enjoyed our first Campsgiving away from family, we were thankful for the company of friends and family over the next two years. And while we put additional pressure on ourselves to host the perfect holiday away from home, we also recognized the time out in the woods had alleviated much of the stress of yearly holiday hosting in our home. Campsgiving was here to stay.

Chapter 24
I Stretch My Vacation Planning Muscles

When one of my 19 younger cousins announced she was getting married in Iowa at the end of June, I decided I was ready to ditch the plans we were already formulating for a Colorado vacation. I hadn't seen many of my aunts and uncles in years. And with my grandmother's steadily declining health making itself more and more apparent, I felt like it was something I both wanted and needed.

There was just one problem. I forgot to run the change of plans by my husband to see what he wanted to do.

The previous summer, we had fulfilled his lifelong dream of camping with his family at Fort Wilderness in Orlando. We spent one week with our elementary children squeezing in as much Disney fun as our family could handle. Our trip home had been full of vacation dreaming. We had proven Jeff and I could plan a nearly two-week camping trip with our camper and kids. And it meant Jeff was ready to keep checking off items from each of our camping bucket lists.

But I also wanted to see my family.

Because I am a notorious conflict avoider, we didn't make actual plans for our summer vacation until well into May, when Jeff begrudgingly said he would take the time off to camp once again in the Midwest.[1] We could camp our way up and back, but I had to do all the

---

1. It wasn't that we didn't ever want to return "home" to visit family. But as I've said, the move to Texas had opened new doors, and we were hungry for both independence and new experiences. That meant looking for vacations in places outside of the Midwest.

planning. And my initial dreams of adding Minnesota to our camping map had to be scratched. He drew the line at driving the camper that far.

So, with one month to go and the school year finally behind me, I mapped out our trip, made reservations, and waited for the moment we could pack up and go back up north and toward the Midwest for the third summer in a row.[2] This would be our first real cross-country road trip experience, and I was ready to face the challenge.

Our usual practice when driving through Arkansas had always been to follow the GPS, staying on the main roads and stopping at an off-the-highway RV park when Jeff couldn't drive anymore. I decided this time, if this was going to be an actual vacation, we were going to stop at places that felt like vacation stops. The Arkansas State Park system had treated us well during the previous spring break when we spent a few days exploring Hot Springs National Park. It was time to let the state parks do the same for our trip back to the Midwest.

Thankfully, while it was a long first day, we arrived at White Oak Lake State Park in Arkansas with plenty of time to spare before the sun went down. Jeff backed into our spot. I took Lydia to the bathroom. And Jeff and Ethan started setting up camp. Lydia and I returned from our bathroom break to find my little seven-year-old walking around with a power drill like the little man he desperately wanted to be.

With the camper safely parked, I promptly sent our kids to the nearby playground to use up some of the energy that had built up after seven hours in the truck. By the time they returned to our campsite, frozen pulled pork was thawing in a pot of boiling water. I sent them back out on their bikes, telling them it was the perfect loop for them to ride.

---

2. The previous summer we had driven up to Indianapolis for our niece/goddaughter's baptism. Since Jeff was already taking time off for a family trip to Disney, he couldn't take more time off to stay. The kids and I spent extra time in Indiana before driving home to Houston in time to prepare for our official family vacation.

The campground sits on the edge of a lake, and both kids wanted to check out the docks. Since I usually got nervous at the idea of my kids being unsupervised around water, I told them I preferred they wait for Jeff or me to explore that area with them. But Lydia, now a determined nine-year-old, insisted she could handle the trip across the campground to the lake by herself. I was stirring the pulled pork when I heard what sounded like our daughter's scream.

"Did that sound like Lydia?" I turned to ask Jeff.

"Maybe. But we would hear more if there was something wrong, right?" Jeff's voice was confident, and he went back to resting in his camp chair after the long drive. But I wasn't sure.

I hopped onto my bike, riding around the loop until I found our little girl, sitting on the ground at the bottom of a hill next to a set of trash cans. She was surrounded by two strangers helping to comfort her while she inspected her own body. Still not fully skilled at speed control on hills, she hadn't slowed down enough as she went downhill and experienced her first big bike crash. With a minor scrape on her knee and both elbows, a huge scrape on her right side where she landed on the ground, and battle scars on her bike helmet and cheek, she was a mess. One of the kind strangers offered to help us get our bikes back to our site and I slowly guided her home, checking out her wounds as we walked.

Our kids were becoming experts at starting road trips with a bang.

By the time Lydia was done eating, she was ready for a family walk to the docks she had tried to visit on her bike. The short stroll to the lake helped highlight what stops at roadside RV parks never revealed to us in the previous three years: the beauty of "The Natural State." There we saw a beautiful natural landscape that rivaled what we had seen further east in Tennessee and Kentucky. The mist hovered over the lake in wisps that only slightly obscured the pine-covered shoreline.

The next day we quickly packed up after a simple breakfast and a short stop down at the visitor's center. Back on the road, Jeff had to drive us through the mountains to the Missouri border, finally getting to Sam A. Baker State Park after another six hours on the road. It was our first stop at a Missouri state park. The campsite was a quick setup, and as soon as I had his bike out of his bedroom, Ethan put on his helmet and started riding the loops. When he asked for a pre-dinner excursion, Jeff and I happily agreed. Easy dinner prep of hot dogs and baked beans could wait until we returned from our ride.

Lydia, still a little wary of jumping on her bike and desperate for some alone time, refused to join us. So our son got some treasured Mommy and Daddy time with just the three of us. He couldn't have been happier. After riding around the camping loop, we decided to give the one-and-a-half-mile bike trail a try, just to see how far he would be able to go. A couple of weeks earlier, when Lydia was at summer camp and Jeff was traveling for work, Ethan and I had attempted a short bike ride around our neighborhood. With the temperatures climbing towards 90 degrees, high humidity, and improperly inflated bike tires, he was done in just a few blocks. So I didn't have high expectations for our family bike ride.

I was wrong.

It was at least ten degrees cooler than when Ethan and I attempted our neighborhood ride and his tire problem had been fixed. He raced over the gravel covering our loop.

We rode along the perfectly smooth bike trail with small rises and dips, the river running through the park to our left as we rode towards the other main camping loop. When we arrived at the next campground over, he insisted we ride around that loop before heading back to our camper. We had logged at least five miles of biking by the time we returned.

I started setting up for dinner, getting the supplies necessary for Jeff and Ethan to make a quick meal of hot dogs, when Jeff said, "Sarah, look up."

I lifted my eyes to see a deer in the empty campsite across from us, peacefully looking for food, oblivious to the growing audience that had just noticed its presence. I got Ethan's attention and he ran inside the camper to get his sister. Both children quietly rushed out and then stood in hushed awe. We watched our animal-loving city girl creep out to the end of our site, longing to pet the wild animal while maintaining a safe, parent-approved distance. This was something new for both of our children, certainly not the kind of thing they would see if we had been staying in a hotel for the night.

After dinner, Lydia agreed to a short ride to prove she wasn't afraid of her bike. We rode over to the visitor center where we parked our bikes.

Our kids did what they do best: they explored. They hopped rocks and eventually fell into the nearby river. Lydia lost a flip-flop, and Jeff chased the runaway shoe while wearing his hard-soled bike sandals. When bedtime stories were finally read and we were able to relax outside with the kids comfortably in bed, it was fair to say we had made the most of our Missouri stop.

Next, we drove through Illinois farmland, cornfield after cornfield with an occasional line of windmills blanketing the landscape.

Then we arrived at Starved Rock State Park, a park Jeff and I had enjoyed years earlier when we tent-camped there with one of his friends from work. Our camping neighbor helped us navigate into a difficult, tree-lined site. Once we finally had the camper parked, Lydia grabbed the map and found the camp playground. She and her brother played until dinner, then returned again only when Jeff went to bring them back for bedtime.

Three days into our trip and our kids were in full camping mode.

We interrupted their play the next morning to head to the state park visitor center, just to see what was there before leaving for our next stop. Jeff and I had 15-year-old memories of a full weekend of beautiful hikes to cliffs and waterfalls, which would have been a lot of fun to try with our kids. But with another 200 miles before our next stop, we only had enough time for the kids to ooh and ahh over the informative visitor center exhibits and for Jeff to give in to one very short hike up to the top of Starved Rock.

We then headed toward Wisconsin, passing rolling midwestern fields of corn and soy and crossing the Mississippi for the second and then third time of our trip up north. Finally, we arrived at Nelson Dewey State Park for two full days and three nights, before a short drive to Dubuque for my cousin's wedding.

At Nelson Dewey, there was no playground, but our kids found a puddle and started making their own dirty fun. They played with chalk, worked on crafting a dirt pile, and made a "potion" in a pothole using dirt, a stick, and a water bottle they took from the truck.

After dinner, I taught our children how to take showers in the campground's cold push-button shower, a new experience for both kids.

When we woke up to the coolest temperatures we had experienced in months, I was ready for a day of actual vacationing instead of hooking up the camper so we could travel to a new campsite in a new state. But first I needed to refill our propane tanks.[3]

When I pulled up to the one store that promised the possibility of propane, I had a pleasant conversation with the only person in the store who promised if I wanted to leave the tanks and pay for them, she would put our names on them and then put them in the alley. Just that simple. After years of living in big cities, this honest and open small-town friendliness felt a little too good to be true. But when we got back from adventuring, those propane tanks were waiting for us in the back alley, just as she had promised.[4]

We spent the morning hiking in the state park. Then we drove to Potosi, Wisconsin, for lunch and a museum tour at Potosi Brewing

---

3. We needed the propane for cooking and heating our water. We also used propane to turn on the heat when it got too cold, but that wasn't a concern during the summer months.

4. Nelson Dewey State Park is located just outside of a small town known for its ferry, which runs back and forth across the Mississippi River, and the festivals it holds throughout the year. It's not quite a "blink and you'll miss it" small town, but pretty close. It was clear it was the kind of town where everyone knew each other and didn't worry about leaving their doors locked.

Company. The afternoon was spent hiking and exploring back across the Mississippi River at Effigy Mounds National Monument in Iowa.

Finally, it was time to head toward the chaos that would be the next couple of days of extended family and wedding celebration. We pulled into the county park campground and Jeff parked the camper in a single try. When my sister Rachel and her family finally arrived at the campground so they could join us over the next two days, we figured out where to place the additional tent and then got the stuff inside our camper so three of their four kids could help test the sleeping limits of our camper.

For the next two days, we hung out with my sisters and their kids, happy to watch all of our offspring enjoying their cousins while I enjoyed getting caught up with my large extended family. The first night we had most of my immediate family over for a couple of hours of campfire fun and conversation, and the next morning we took advantage of the hotel pool where over half of the wedding attendees were staying. Ethan and one nephew, who is six months older, and another nephew, who is six months younger, played like there had never been a gap in their time together. And each night we got to return to our home turf, not a hotel, and know we were sleeping in our beds with our kids and nieces and nephew in the next room over, happily enjoying the chance to spend extra time together.

Even at a county park, during a camping stop when we didn't have much time for "camping" activities, our kids still found the time to wonder at nature. They chased fireflies and enjoyed bare feet in the fire ant-free grass.[5] They went into the river that ran through the county park. And they played without the concerns of disturbing hotel guests.

We left the evening before we originally planned, with the goal of getting through most of Iowa for our first night on the road. We found a roadside RV park which worked out perfectly, until the next

---

5. Walking in the grass with bare feet in Texas is always a risk, because a fire ant mound can develop anywhere.

morning, when I was awakened at 6 AM by countless tiny thuds and pecks. At first, I thought the kids were up, but when I went in to check on them, they were both still asleep in their beds. I thought maybe we had a wild animal in our camper, but that didn't make sense either. Then I opened up the door. A full flock of birds flew away from around our camper, filling the field next to the campground. I walked around the camper just to make sure that we didn't have any lingering visitors, and finally fell back asleep so that I could at least pretend to be well-rested before we got on the road.

We spent the next night at Land of the Ozarks State Park in Missouri. We arrived at the state park with enough time for the kids to swim in the lake before we broke one of our cardinal rules for camping and headed to the local Steak N' Shake.[6]

While our trip to Iowa had not been a dream vacation, it certainly had me dreaming about the future. That night, I shocked Jeff by suggesting maybe we should start looking for a new camper.

I loved the moving hotel room that had traveled over fifteen thousand miles with us over the previous four years. It had been our home away from home and gotten us through the first six difficult weeks of our move to Houston as we were waiting for our house to be available. But the trip to Wisconsin and back, with multiple stops and starts in less than two weeks, had demonstrated to us what six weeks of living in it had not: as our family grew up, we needed a camper that would give us the space to spread out and grow as a family as well.

Our final night away ended up being a planned stop at a KOA in Oklahoma, as we decided to take the long drive straight home instead of stopping for one more night. The discussion about a new camper

---

6. The dealer who sold us the Roo had told us years before that his family never ate in the campground, something we couldn't even begin to comprehend. As a result, we were determined to prove we could almost always eat at the campground. We've continued to maintain this practice on nearly every vacation since that first summer of camper ownership.

continued between Jeff and me as we loaded back into the truck the next morning.

I was ready to be home. A month later, we would sell the Gray Wolf and upgrade one more time to our slightly bigger Imagine.

For years Jeff and I had been dreaming about big, long national park trips with the camper. While he didn't want to take the Iowa trip, it taught us how to do long trips. The vacation taught me how to plan stops and menus and activities along the way.

We were finally prepared to do more. And so we did.

Chapter 25
Christmas Break in the Texas Mountains

WHEN WE RETURNED FROM a family vacation to the Midwest for my cousin's wedding, I took a deep breath.

I needed a vacation from my so-called vacation.

I had a wonderful time visiting family; we had seen and done some fun things. But by the last day of our vacation, I was pulling out the map and looking at the match-up of national and state parks in Texas, determined to explore with just the four of us before the end of 2018.

By the end of July, I had mapped out a Christmas break trip to southwest Texas with stays near Fort Davis and Big Bend National Park. Jeff approved the plans and I made reservations. For months we looked forward to the end-of-year trip. When the stress from work and school and life stretched us to our limit, Jeff and I held on to that planned week of camping far away in the middle of the Texas desert.

But then, in early December, the news outlets were flooded with the possibility of a government shutdown. My brain, which was already overloaded with end-of-the-semester responsibilities, was suddenly overrun with a series of what-ifs related to our Christmas break plans. For ten days we waited on pins and needles for every piece of news related to what was happening in Washington, D.C. And I completely ignored the other potential problem: a camper that was still in the shop for repairs for warranty issues we had discovered during our latest Campsgiving trip.

By December 21st, I was checking the Facebook page for Big Bend to see what kind of notifications they might be posting in case of a government shutdown. But the park was ignoring the potential disturbance during one of the biggest visitor seasons of the year. Instead, they warned potential visitors to "plan on a busy park during the Christmas and New Year's week." The page exploded with comments from many who were plannin a visit, including us.

And then at midnight—shutdown.

I have a tendency to worst-case scenario a situation over which I have no control. I started searching for other options for camping in Texas, fully aware that most, if not all, state park campgrounds were full for the coming week. I found a couple of available campsites and went to tell Jeff what I had found.

He pulled me onto his lap, looked me in the eye, and said, "We're not going on this trip to get stamps. We're going so we can be together as a family. It will be okay, even if it won't be exactly as you planned it."

I will never stop being thankful for a husband who knows how to settle me down when my brain goes spiraling out of control.

With all of our actual camping plans unaffected by the shutdown, we agreed to make the best of an imperfect situation.

But the camper was still in the shop. When I called on Christmas Eve morning, they were still waiting on the part for the sink, the only thing that *needed* to be fixed before we headed down the road for a week. Our excited kids repeatedly asked about everything related to Christmas Eve, including when we were going to open presents. The problem? Every single plan for Christmas Eve Day hinged on when we were going to be able to pick up the camper. Until we knew that, we didn't know which church service we would be attending, when we were going to eat both lunch and dinner, and when we would be opening presents. I found myself yelling at our kids nearly every ten to 15 minutes to stop asking me questions, each question raising my anxiety and turning me into a Grinch who was stealing their Christmas joy.

After hours of waiting for the repair shop to finish, we were finally able to bring the camper home.

The rest of Christmas Eve was a whirlwind, including seven-year-old Ethan asking me to tell him the truth about who filled their stockings.

"What do *you* think?" I asked, trying to stave off the inevitable.

His big hazel eyes searched mine. "I want you to tell me the truth. Is Santa real?"

I let out a big sigh and cobbled together some version of the truth and Christmas magic. Satisfied with my answer, Ethan promptly ignored my directive to *not* tell his older sister, and I had to have the whole conversation over again before they both went to sleep.

But Christmas Day was a fresh start. Texas is so big it was going to take us two days of driving to get to Davis Mountains, so we spent our first night in Garner State Park. The next morning we woke up to rain and wind that followed us the rest of our trip west.

It didn't take long after leaving Garner before we began to see border patrol agents, then cars with Mexico license plates, and finally Border Control Checkpoints. It was clear we were getting closer to the border, but we were still more than an hour's drive away. We did get to experience our first-ever Border Control Checkpoint, watching a German Shepherd and his human agent companion walk around our truck and camper before we were quickly released to continue on our way.

Over the next several hours we watched the landscape change from the hill country to the wide-open desert and then to mountains growing up around us. We finally arrived at Davis Mountains State Park before sunset and settled in.

When I left the camper that night to walk to the bathroom, I looked up and all I saw were stars. The Big Dipper was clear as day right in front of us. I called the rest of the family outside so that they could also take in the starry night. The kids complained about the cold, but those complaints died down as Jeff and I pointed out just how many stars they could see in the dark campground. Light pollution was completely nonexistent in the middle of the desert mountains.

We woke up the next morning ready to explore. After taking care of a few errands, Jeff drove to the overlook at the top of Skyline Drive. There were mountaintops all around us when Ethan exclaimed, "I've always wanted to see a mountain!" It was clear that awe of the mountain peaks took some of the edge off the 40-degree temperatures with an even colder windchill. Lydia distracted herself by jumping from rock to rock, ignoring the drop-off on all sides of the mountain peak and exclaiming her own love for the rugged terrain.

By the time one of the park rangers showed up for the 11 AM interpretive talk, "Sky Island Party," I wasn't sure the kids would want to endure the cold wind any longer. But Ranger Ty pulled out leis and the kids were game. This was how we learned that the Davis Mountains is one of three "islands in the sky" in the state of Texas—Guadalupe Mountains and Chisos Basin in Big Bend being the other two. This would inspire us to hike in the Guadalupe Mountains six months later.

After our ranger-led nature experience in the mountain-top wind, the whole family was cold and hungry. Instead of heading back for sandwiches at the camper, we went to the Civilian Conservation Corps-constructed Indian Lodge on the other side of the state park for lunch at their tiny restaurant. It almost felt like tradition as Jeff and I thought back to the very different CCC-constructed Potawatomi Inn in Pokagon State Park in Indiana.[1]

When we finally returned to our camper, the kids took off for the dry creek bed below the campsite to play with the rocks. With the winter temperatures, I had few concerns about snakes and scorpions, so I let them go crazy. They made rock sculptures and found treasures galore.

---

1. The Civilian Conservation Corps, or CCC, was a 1930s work program that transformed our national and state park systems. Many of the state parks we loved in both Indiana and Texas were built by the CCC. The more we have explored the United States, the more we have seen the lasting power of the program in both our state and national parks.

But Jeff and I weren't done exploring. We leashed up the dogs and walked as a family to the base of the Montezuma Quail Trail, a nearly two-mile hike up the mountainside over rocky trails, taking a 220-foot climb in elevation at the highest point. As we started our ascent, Ethan exclaimed, "I've always wanted to climb a mountain." We seemed to be accomplishing all of his little dreams in one day.

The day was almost over, but I wanted to watch a western sunset. The top of the Skyline Drive overlook hadn't gotten any warmer over the day, the cold wind still cutting across the top of the peak, but the changing colors over the mountainous desert landscape were more breathtaking than the wind. We waited with the few other families who chose to brave the cold and watched as the sun slowly went over the mountain.

The clear, cold night sky presented another perfect view of the stars. The whole day in the mountains may have been colder than we Houston transplants had become accustomed to, but the refreshing time outside made it all worth it. Thankful for a heated camper, we snuggled into our beds to prepare for a trip down south the next day.

Big Bend National Park was always supposed to be the crown jewel of our Christmas camping vacation. Located in the desolate southwestern corner of Texas, it isn't as popular as Arches or Yellowstone, but the park's biodiversity and relatively mild winter climate make it a popular winter location. Yes, I wanted to check another national park off of the list. But I also wanted to camp close so we could hike, stargaze, and cross the Rio Grande into Mexico at the Boquillas border crossing.[2] I wanted to see everything the park had to offer.

When the shutdown happened, I was convinced even if we still visited the park, it was going to be a mere shadow of what our original planned trip was going to be. The visitor centers were all closed, the border crossing was closed, and other facilities throughout the

---

2. We even made a special family trip to downtown Houston after an October soccer game to get our passports in preparation for the border crossing that wouldn't happen.

park were unsupervised. We wouldn't get stamps, the kids wouldn't be able to do the Junior Ranger program, and we didn't know what the bathroom situation would be by the time we arrived in the park. But despite the uncertainty, I still wanted to take the trek south.

We had already decided to stay in Davis Mountains for our entire vacation, letting go of our plan to pack up and head south for two nights outside of the national park. Then I checked the forecast. The day I had originally scheduled for exploring the park, the temperatures were supposed to drop by at least 20 degrees from the 60-degrees forecasted for our second full day in Davis Mountains. So instead of another day hiking in Davis Mountains, we headed 100 miles south for a day in the national park.

The next morning, we didn't quite get an eight o'clock start time for our long day of travel, but we were close enough. By the time we left, the sun was starting to rise over the mountains.

When we finally arrived in Terlingua/Study Butte, the last stop before the national park, we discovered we had stopped at the gas station right next to the RV resort where we had a reservation. I hadn't been able to cancel our reservation because I didn't have enough cell service to make a phone call, so we walked into the office/gift shop to see what we could do. The desk clerk cheerfully greeted us and after we explained our situation, he gladly returned our deposit even though we had clearly missed our 72-hour cancellation window. Many of the people who had been kicked out of the national park due to shutdown closures had turned to the surrounding RV parks for replacement lodging. Our cancellation would open up a spot for another family looking for a place to stay now that they couldn't stay in the park.

Following the recommendation of the desk clerk, we headed into the park and straight for Chisos Basin Lodge, an independently run establishment inside the national park that still had an open gift shop, restaurant, and restrooms. On the way there, we watched the desert shift to the mountains again, vegetation getting denser and trees taller while we felt the elevation change. We pulled into a full

Chisos Basin complex, cars and trucks parked on the road and hikers and tourists crossing parking lots to get to their desired location. Our kids watched in awe as they passed license plates from all over the country, national park lovers determined to not let a shutdown keep them from exploring one of the less frequently visited parks in the United States during its traditionally busiest time of the year.

We made a quick stop through the gift shop, returned to the truck to get water bottles and Jeff's hiking boots, and then headed down to the hiking trails. Lydia and Ethan, oblivious to the other hikers around them and the trail sign ahead of them, were immediately distracted by the warning sign giving instructions on how to avoid bears and mountain lions. When we finally got their attention, we let them take a look at the sign and pick the trail. Already hungry and asking when lunch would be, they picked the shortest of the trails, the almost-two-mile Chisos Basin Loop.[3] We fed them snacks along the way, my desire for a family hike overshadowing their desire for food.

We climbed, stepped over rocks, and steadied ourselves as we made each descent. We started to shed layers of clothing no longer necessary once our blood was pumping. The kids, distracted by the possibility of wildlife and the mountain views, forgot they were hungry until near the end of the hike. When we finally returned to the store at the trailhead, we guzzled multiple glasses of water and devoured our lunch at the Chisos Basin Restaurant, the food fueling us up for a second round.

We said goodbye to the Basin and traveled toward the Rio Grande Village. From the top of the Rio Grande Overlook we could see into Mexico and the pangs of being so close but so far away hit us as we looked across the rugged wilderness.

As far as I was concerned, the day had been nearly perfect, but I still hadn't seen the Rio Grande. And Ethan still hadn't *really* seen Mexico.

---

3. The loop had an elevation of 350 feet, took us through forests and past cacti and delivered spectacular views of the mountains and valley below.

He wanted to be able to brag to his friends that we'd gone to another country. I just wanted to know what we were missing with the closed border crossing.

On our way back to Panther Junction, Jeff pulled off toward the Hot Springs historic site, taking our truck on the bumpy dirt road and then the incredibly narrow one-way road leading to the parking lot right next to the Langford Ruins on the top of a hill. We headed down the quarter-mile hike toward the natural hot springs pool, and then I heard it: the rushing waters of the Rio Grande to our right. Our son raced down the trail to the hot springs. The break in the bamboo growing on the banks revealed a small stone pool full of naturally heated water, the pristine frigid waters of the Rio Grande running right past it. Park visitors filled the pool, braving the sixty-degree weather to don their swimming suits and enjoy the warm water. Some of them took advantage of the ranger-less park to dive from the hot spring to the icy river water beyond it. Both of our kids took off their shoes and socks so they could put their feet in, Lydia stretching her long legs off the edge of the pool so she could dip her toes into the Rio Grande.

It was our last stop inside Big Bend. Once we left the park, we made a quick stop in Terlingua Ghost Town, staying long enough to visit the gift shop and the old cemetery on our way out of town. On the way home, an icy fog settled around the truck; we still had nearly an hour to go and we could barely see in front of us.

As I tucked our excitable little boy into bed, he told me he couldn't settle down. In his words, he "didn't want the fun to end."

That statement pretty much summed up the day.

On our last full day in Davis Mountains, the kids decided to make our wedding anniversary special. By the time I returned from walking both dogs around the loop and pouring two pots of boiling water over the frozen water spout, they had attempted to make Jeff and me breakfast, complete with coffee. I gladly ate my Cornflakes with just a little too much milk.

Thanks to the temperature drop, we spent much of the day inside, playing games and eventually turning on the television so Jeff could watch Michigan play in a bowl game.

When Jeff and I walked down to the gift shop at the Indian Lodge, a brochure inspired us to finish our stay in the Davis Mountains with a trip up the road to the McDonald Observatory to take in their nightly Star Party.

The overcast skies never cleared for the telescopes, but we sat inside the warm visitor center and listened to one of the astronomers talk about the various constellations that can be viewed at the observatory, complete with pictures and diagrams. Then we braved the 22-degree mountain temperatures to look at two of the telescopes they use for viewing at the visitor center before exploring the much warmer indoor exhibit for ourselves.

And while it could have scared us from ever returning, the light dusting of snow on the ground was the icing on the cake of our first-ever Christmas break camping trip. I couldn't wait to plan the next one.

Chapter 26

"Dad, do I have to turn myself in?"

When we moved to Texas, we had to change our approach to Memorial Day weekend camping. Every year for five years, my teaching job required participation in the graduation ceremony that took place at the beginning of the weekend, which meant we couldn't travel far. And by the end of May, Texas was already hot; temperatures below 70 didn't reappear until late September. We also had to plan well in advance, because our favorite nearby state parks were usually booked for holiday weekends six months out.

But in 2019, we planned well in advance. Since Huntsville State Park was just over an hour from our house, we could still camp there during Memorial Day weekend. I would be able to drive the hour back to northwest Harris County to attend the evening ceremony while my family enjoyed some time camping in Texas before the summer swelter really set in. We hadn't been camping since our short spring break trip to Bastrop State Park, just outside of Austin. Jeff and I were ready to shake out some of the cobwebs before our big summer vacation.

The weekend plans got off to a rough start. When we arrived at the camper storage, we discovered the camper's battery was dead. Instead of hooking up the camper and packing food and clothes in front of our house the night before leaving, we would have to wait nearly twenty-four hours until we were all home from our final day of school.[1] The next day would be a mad rush to finish the packing so that we could be in Huntsville well before evening.

It didn't get better after our arrival at the state park. For the first time ever, we intentionally parked twice, deciding we were too far off level after the first attempt to be satisfied for the next three days. We hooked back up, moved the leveling blocks, and parked again, somehow doing it without arguing with each other, taking the change in parked position in stride. While I headed back toward Houston for my high school's graduation ceremony, Jeff and the kids enjoyed an easy dinner before biking around the campground and checking out the friendly neighborhood alligators hanging out under the fishing pier attached to our campground loop.

Everyone woke up the next morning with different plans. I made breakfast, dreaming of a morning hike. Lydia begged me to ride with her to the main office to pick up a Texas Junior Ranger backpack. When we finally returned, both kids sorted through the items in the bag, distracted long enough for Jeff and I to take a quick bike ride to the lake recreational area. Our kids were just starting to get old enough that we could leave them for short bursts, and we certainly felt better leaving them alone in the state park. Jeff has always loved driving or riding around campgrounds to see how other people have set up their sites or what equipment they have brought along. I enjoyed the rare opportunity to ride my bike without worrying about kids and cars. Together we enjoyed just a few minutes of alone time before heading back to the noise and excitement that was two kids and two dogs at our campsite.

I finally got my family hike *after* lunch. The Prairie Branch Loop took us along the lake and through wooded forests, pine, oak, and elm trees reaching into the sky above us. The kids stopped every

---

1. One of the unfortunate realities of living in our subdivision in Houston was we didn't have a good place to park our camper without irritating the homeowners association. We're thankful that our last two Indiana houses have provided us the space to leave the camper at home with us.

five minutes for a water break and to glance through wildflower and dragonfly guides to decipher everything they saw. Ethan hit his hiking stick along the boarded walks under the guise of scaring away venomous snakes. Lydia took charge of their backpack so she could lead the way, telling us that we had to stay behind them for the duration of the trail. Her long, blonde braids swung at her sides while Ethan's blue hat flopped with each jump on the boards and over roots.

Despite the kids' insistence that we take frequent water breaks, the heat took every ounce of energy we all had left. Our camper's air-conditioning made us thankful that we had left the tent camping days behind us. Revived, Ethan convinced me to ride our bikes over to the camp store to buy fishing worms and check out the small inlet beach.[2]

There were already *so* many people swimming in the water and sitting on towels and blankets placed on the coarse sand. With it being Memorial Day weekend and only an hour north of the Houston metropolitan area, I knew that number would only grow during the weekend.

"How does the beach look?" Jeff asked when we returned.

"Crowded," I said. I didn't really want to go swimming at the small beach. But I knew the murky water would cool us all off, and the local alligators stayed away from that part of the lake. "Let's go. We need to get out of the camper."

For the next hour, Jeff and I went back and forth between hanging out in the shallow water and watching our kids swim and dig in the sand. The cool water felt good, especially as the sun baked on my skin. It wasn't Lake Michigan, but it would do for the weekend, and that was all I could ask for.

---

2. Texas state parks allow visitors to fish for free in all of the state parks. During the years we lived there, Jeff and both kids enjoyed multiple trips to lakes to cast a line and catch and release.

After dinner, Ethan dragged Jeff down to the dock to fish. Lydia watched her little brother catch and release at least one fish, while her hook remained untouched. I stood along the railing and watched as the resident alligators swam back and forth underneath the dock.

"Mom, I'm bored. Can we go back to the camper?" The light in Lydia's eyes dimmed after her failed fishing expedition.

"Sure, honey. Want to make some s'mores?"

"Yes!"

It was too hot for a campfire, so I turned on the pellet grill and placed the marshmallows, graham crackers, and chocolate onto a roasting pan, waiting for the marshmallows to puff up to perfect, melted goodness. The result wasn't *quite* what we would get with a fire-roasted marshmallow, but the chocolate and sugar helped erase Lydia's disappointment. That short, quiet moment with just the two of us raised her spirits enough that she was ready to eagerly welcome her brother and dad back after they were done on the docks.

Even after a night of fishing, Ethan still wasn't done. The next morning he dragged Jeff out of bed extra early for some morning fishing. While the boys fished, Lydia and I filled our water bottles and hiked the Dogwood Trail.

We walked under the leafy green canopy and stepped over roots as Lydia chattered away between water breaks.

"Mom, what makes a bad word a 'bad' word?"

"Why don't people care about global warming?"

"Why did God make people if He knew that we were just going to screw it all up?"

My ten-year-old wanted to talk about everything from the musical *Hamilton* to animal conservation and her desire to save *all* of the animals she possibly could. In the safety of the woods, I relished the not-so-quiet time with my girl, hopeful that she would always feel like she could talk to me that freely. With puberty knocking on the door, I hoped I had laid enough groundwork during our time together. I didn't want these heart-to-heart conversations to ever disappear.

After lunch, our kids entertained themselves inside the camper, enjoying the air conditioning instead of braving the heat. The camper bounced as they played games in their bedroom and it was hard to tell if the constant indoor shrieking and yelling was out of happiness or anger. We frustratedly kicked the kids out, giving them the choice between dishes and playing at the playground. I also wanted them to experience more freedom and independence in the safety of the campground. They were getting older. They were ready for more responsibility and the autonomy exploring on their own would give them. Besides, I figured if they were together, they could look out for each other.

Forty-five minutes later, an upset Ethan returned telling us, "You kicked us out of the camper and we got lost." They got turned around while on their bikes and were temporarily uncertain about where they were going, but they were never lost. Jeff and I tried to keep our faces straight as we repeatedly pointed out that they had learned important life lessons and they still got "home" safely, completely unharmed, although recovering from the stress of forced independence. But once they were out of earshot, we looked at each other and started laughing. We didn't want to mock our son's genuine distress, but we wanted to challenge them to be more independent and take more relatively low risks. I also knew that I would have been far more distraught if they hadn't made it back, and I breathed an inward sigh of relief that, in the end, no harm was done.

To get their minds off of the mishap, we spent the late afternoon once again cooling off in the lake, both kids building sculptures and waterways with their hands and the beach toys that another little girl had the foresight to bring along. Jeff and I finally convinced the kids it was time for dinner, Ethan encouraged to leave with the promise he could go fishing one more time.

I may not have been a patient fishing bystander, but I entertained myself with alligator viewing. As I sat on the deck waiting for my family to catch a fish, I made myself a one-person gator sighting welcoming committee, helping fellow campers find the lonely swimmer so they could get pictures. Eventually, he was joined by two companions eager to grab fish swimming for the hooks dangling in the water.

Lydia was the first one to give up. "Mom, I'm ready to go home."

"Are you sure?"

She sighed, her body language full of disappointment with her failure to catch fish and annoyance at watching her little brother successfully catch a few small ones. "Yes."

A short while later, Ethan returned without Jeff, leaving his dad to clean up the fishing equipment on his own. Lydia stubbornly decided to not be outdone by her brother. She headed back to the dock, intercepting Jeff right before he left the pier. Since Ethan had finished off the worms, Jeff asked a fellow camper if they could have a single nightcrawler. Our little conservationist caught a small catfish on the first try. Thrilled that she had caught something yet determined to let the catfish live to see another day, she got help taking it off the hook and threw it back into the lake, only to watch the freed fish get gobbled by one of the three gators that called the pier cove home.

Her excitement over the successful catch and horror over the catfish's untimely demise was amplified when she realized she had just inadvertently fed an alligator.

Eyes wide, they flashed back and forth between Jeff and a sign specifically stating a hefty fine for feeding the alligators. Her voice wavering, Lydia said, "Dad, do I have to turn myself in?"

With both kids in bed, Jeff filled insulated cups with ice and handed me a rare margarita, a reward for a day of hiking and exploring and wrangling our crew. Jeff and I walked around the loop one last time, stopping at the end of the pier to enjoy the breeze over the open water. I laughed as he relayed the story of Lydia feeding the alligator, unconcerned that our daughter would turn into a hardened criminal. We enjoyed the quiet, kid-free conversation and returned to our home-away-from-home ready for some much-needed sleep.

The weekend wasn't perfect. It was still really hot. Ethan had a couple of heat rash outbreaks. Lydia came home with a headache, and both kids had inexplicable ornery moments that left us looking at each other wondering what more we could possibly do to help them turn their emotions around.

Thankfully, we weren't looking for perfection; we were looking to build memories and moments together as a family.

Chapter 27
Guano Happens

As meaningful as our Iowa trip had been for me, when we returned home in 2018, Jeff and I were desperate to plan a vacation that checked off dream national parks. Mesa Verde and Arches National Park had been on my "bucket list" since I was a teenager and Jeff was ready to give both a chance, especially since living in southeast Texas put us closer to the American Southwest. I started plotting out the best route that would allow us to visit as many national parks as possible between Houston and Moab, Utah, in the allotted time Jeff had given me: two weeks.

After months of drafting plans, handing them to Jeff, and him paring them down to something more reasonable, we could not wait for our summer 2019 national parks adventure to begin.

We traveled across Texas, spending our first night in South Llano State Park where the kids swam and played in the comfortably cool knee-high rapids of the river, letting the water sweep them to the boundaries we had set and then fighting those same rapids to get back to where they had started. Jeff and I stood in the cool, rushing water and then worked our way to a rock island so we could watch the activity from there.

We spent our second night still in Texas, the sand dunes of Monahans Sandhills State Park rising behind our campsite. Our kids couldn't get enough of the sand, regardless of the dry heat and biting flies. They attempted to build sand castles that fell apart as soon as they were formed and then later eagerly climbed from one dune peak to the next, JT and Bella bounding behind them after Jeff took off the dog's leashes so they too could enjoy the cooling sand between their toes.

The next day we enjoyed a much shorter drive across the New Mexico border to Brantley Lake State Park, our base camp for exploring Guadalupe Mountains and Carlsbad Caverns.

Lydia had been begging to visit Guadalupe Mountains National Park since our Christmas break trip to Davis Mountains State Park the previous December. A combination of fourth grade Texas state history and learning about islands in the sky from a park ranger in Davis Mountains convinced her that seeing the tallest point in Texas needed to be on her wish list for the near future. I also had vague memories of driving through the park when I was in high school while on a youth ministry travel team, the only evidence of our stop a group picture in front of El Capitan, so I was eager to actually spend time in the park.

We spent at least two hours at the visitor center, both kids looking through the displays and completing enough activities to earn their first Junior Ranger badge of our vacation. We hiked the short nature trail just behind the visitor center, stamped our passports, and drove a couple of miles down the road for a picnic lunch. The rangers had recommended the picnic area if we wanted a good view of El Capitan, with Guadalupe Peak right behind it.[1] Energized by a food break cut short by an annoying swarm of flies, we headed back north toward the Frijole Ranch Trailhead with plans to hike just over two miles on the moderate Smith Spring Trail so we could see a small waterfall in the middle of the desert.

At least, that was the plan.

Everyone was fully equipped with a filled personal water bottle, hat, and sunglasses. I signed the trail register before we started on our way, which probably should have been the first sign this wasn't going to be a simple trail. It was hot (probably around 95 degrees by

---

1. At 8751 feet, it is the highest point in Texas.

the time we started) and both kids were excitedly rushing ahead of us, but we were still on the trail.

Then everything went completely off of the rails.

The Smith Springs Trail crosses a rocky creek bed which is not marked on the map. When we got to the creek bed, we didn't pay attention to the trail that clearly continued on the other side. Instead, we looked to our left to what appeared to be a marked rocky trail and headed up. For the next 30 minutes, we climbed, ducked under branches, and looked for the clearest route on the rocky path while I kept a close lookout for rattlesnakes and mountain lions.

Eventually, when we got to what appeared to be the top—climbing I don't know how many vertical feet in the process—I climbed out of the creek bed to see if there were any other visible trails, and we decided it was time to turn around. Our return to our original detour revealed our error. To the right was the path we had come from, and to left was the path we were supposed to take. Jeff and I shook our heads at our mistake, both of us accepting part of the blame. The kids joked about how we always tell them to stay on the path, and this time *we* had broken the rules.

Hot and dehydrated, we eventually decided to turn around, never making it to the waterfall, but thankful we had returned safely without any encounter with deadlier desert wildlife in the park beside the mountain lion scat we saw on the trail.

As much as we enjoyed the Guadalupe Mountains, it would pale in comparison to the next day's explorations of Carlsbad National Park.

The first words out of Ethan's mouth when I woke him up the next morning were, "When are we leaving for the caves? We need to leave. I don't want to miss them!" This was a significant contrast to the day before, when he woke up complaining about not wanting to leave the campground so we could drive to Guadalupe.

I laughed as I turned toward the kitchen to start eating my breakfast and making coffee. "Ethan, we can't leave yet. Our tour isn't until 1:30. Bella and JT need us to stick around for a little bit before we leave them for the rest of the day. I promise we aren't going to miss it."

After a short detour around road construction, we arrived at the national park with just enough time to get down the elevator for our tour. Our first tour of the day was the ranger-led King's Palace Tour. The kids asked questions and learned more about the history, exploration, and science of the cave. We appreciated a slower pace with the group as we slowly walked past rooms full of clusters of ivory stalactites descending from a cave ceiling, occasionally breaking up the pattern of Swiss cheese-like holes overhead.

Then the ranger turned off all the lights.

Cave darkness: It can be frightening to not even be able to see your hand in front of your face. All the other senses suddenly wake up and every sound in the cave is amplified. I remember a tour guide at Mammoth Cave talking about the amount of time it takes for someone to lose their mind if they are stuck in a cave without any source of light. It doesn't take a few weeks; it happens in a matter of days. Once you have experienced cave darkness, it is easy to understand how someone could easily lose mental stability, lost in a cave without the ability to see anything, every other sense suddenly more attuned to the sounds, smells, and touch around them. Our guide told us about one particular blind man who had taught himself to use echolocation, just like bats, proving that people can learn to use their other senses and adapt. Suddenly the stories in comic books didn't seem so impossible.

At the end of the tour we had a choice: we could go to the left and climb out of the cave through the Natural Entrance or we could head back up the elevators. We chose to take the elevators up to the top so the kids could go to the bathroom and get sworn in as Junior Rangers, their second badge of the trip. While they were getting sworn in, we heard the announcement that the Natural Entrance was going to be closing in ten minutes. We rushed the kids and ranger through the process and then ran to the Natural Entrance so we could climb down into the cave for a self-guided tour.

The pungent aroma of bat guano grew the closer we got to the entrance and the further we walked down the winding pathway lining the gaping hole in the ground that had been discovered for exploration near the end of the 19th century. The further we walked, the more awed we were by the vastness of the entrance. I was thankful we had opted to climb *down* from the top instead of the other way around.

After climbing down several hundred feet we looked back up to see the dim light still coming from the Natural Entrance, pondering what it must have been like to be one of the first to climb into the cave with no lights in front of us and only light behind us. We walked past the Bat Room, the depths from which the seasonally roosting bats emerged every night. Through the entire trail, we were introduced to an ever-changing world of natural wonders. Within 45 minutes we had descended 750 feet and walked over a mile, meeting up with the Big Room Route at the other end of the cave.

Not to be prevented from doing "all the things," we continued on the self-guided Big Room Route, walking over another mile to see nearly every kind of cave formation, large and small, high and low. The Big Room is just over eight acres of nature at its finest. Large pillars of stalagmites rose from the floor and reached to the ceiling. Stalactites hung in icicle-like clusters. Carefully placed lighting bounced off the ivory mineral formations, giving the appearance of an underground crystal palace. Nearly every step in the cave took my breath away.

We were all hungry and ready to stop climbing by the time we saw the sign for the elevators (three miles of cave hiking is a different experience altogether), but we were fully satisfied with everything we had seen.

We walked out of the doors to the approaching dusk, noticing a small crowd in the parking lot. When we got to the circle, we discovered several park visitors taking pictures of a large tarantula slowly making its way across the parking lot. As I pulled out my own phone to take a picture, I heard Ethan exclaim, "Why don't people just leave him alone? He's trying to get back to his family." Sometimes children have far more wisdom about the natural world than adults.

We ended our evening in the bat amphitheater, where we planned to watch the bats emerge from the Natural Entrance for their nightly feed. As with our experience watching the Mexican free-tailed bats the previous summer in Austin, we watched mesmerized by the black cloud of bats rising out of the cave and disappearing into the night. Their tiny bodies were suspended by flapping wings, several of them taking laps around the human audience before flying off for their nightly feed. After ten minutes of watching them fade into the dusk, we were ready to take our tired crew home so we could relieve our dogs and get to bed in preparation for a day of travel.

I knew our family would enjoy the caves, but I had no idea the impact the stop would have on all of us. It took me a while to figure out the difference between our two favorite cave explorations. Mammoth is magnificent; Carlsbad is stunning. What makes Mammoth unique is the long human history of the cave and the magnificent, large caverns; what makes Carlsbad unique is that it shows in elaborate detail the unique world underground and the creative power of water and minerals. And neither were experiences we would ever forget.

Chapter 28
A Palace in the Cliffs

AFTER TWO DAYS OF TOURING THE CARLSBAD region, it was time to head north. We watched the Chihuahuan Desert transform into the Sangre de Cristo Mountains the closer we got to Santa Fe, where we would be making our first non-state park stop of the trip. We pulled into the Santa Fe KOA, dropped the kids off at the playground, checked in, and were parked and completely set up within thirty minutes. We took the dogs to the small campground dog run and the kids found the game room, keeping themselves entertained until we decided it was time to load back up and head out for a couple of hours of exploring.

Since no one in our family had ever been to Santa Fe, we headed downtown, deciding that an evening of eating out and walking around the city center was a good way to spend our single-night stop. We enjoyed New-Mex cuisine and visited vendors along the city center. We listened to street musicians and took pictures of the historic adobe buildings, enjoying our short stop back in civilization.

The next morning we headed north, the mountains changing to desert and back again as we approached Colorado. As we neared Colorado, we pointed out the snowcapped mountains, which had more summer snow on them than I had ever seen before. Our kids, who saw the Smokies before they were old enough to remember, who had driven through the Ozark mountains multiple times, and who had just seen the Guadalupe Mountains in the middle of the west Texas and southern New Mexico desert, gaped at the majestic mountain ranges of the American West. For the first time, they were seeing portions of the mountain range their mom had fallen in love with when she was eleven.

"Mom," Lydia said. "They are beautiful and so big."

"Can we play in the snow?" Ethan asked.

I laughed. "Probably not. We're not going up to those mountains. We just get to look at them from a distance."

Jeff piloted our way through the foothills and mountains, testing the limits of both truck and camper, before we pulled into the KOA with plenty of time for the kids to get out and play at the playground, for us to easily set up, and for the dogs to get a chance to try the campgrounds three-acre dog park.

That afternoon, we took the short drive to the Mesa Verde Visitor Center to purchase our tour tickets for the next couple of days. Because we got there the night before, we were able to easily book two separate tours, get information on the park, and pick up Junior Ranger books so the kids could start on them whenever they were ready. We then sent the kids to bed with the warning we would have to wake up earlier than usual to make it to our scheduled tours.

And I wasn't missing them.

I don't ever remember *not* loving history. My interests in specific periods and parts of the world may have changed over the years, but I've always been fascinated by the past. By the stories of triumphs and failures, the changes that can be seen when looking at clothing and architecture over the years, and the lessons to be learned from studying the lives of people from all cultures and eras.

Ever since high school, when I learned a place existed in the United States where I could see the architectural feats of people who lived

800 years ago, I had wanted to see the cliff dwellings of Mesa Verde for myself.[1]

For nearly 20 years, before I even knew I would want to camp my way across the country, I frequently mentioned my dream to my poor boyfriend, then husband, who always responded with an indication of "someday."

I finally decided that "someday" was the summer of 2019.

I woke up the next morning, excitedly filled water bottles, then extra jugs, packed lunches, and impatiently waited for the rest of my family to be ready to leave our campsite. When we were finally on the road and in the park, Jeff began the slow climb into the mountains, weaving back and forth on the switchbacks. We traveled past more views of snowcapped mountains, valleys, and rocky cliffs. Jeff tried his hardest to keep his eyes on the road while the rest of us oohed and awed at the magical views on each side of the truck.

Jeff laughed at me. "Honey, you are giddy. I think you're more excited than the kids," he said as he snapped a picture of me smiling and holding my coffee mug. And I *was* giddy. I couldn't stop smiling. I was in one of my favorite states in the United States and I was fulfilling a dream. I was normally a war history buff, which is how Jeff convinced me to go to Gettysburg many years before. But this was a window into a magical past, people who had left an architectural wonder and then disappeared. There was hope and mystery in the story of cliff dwellings. I wanted to learn everything I could.

We pulled into the parking lot to meet our ranger and the large group taking the Balcony House tour. Both of the tours we were taking had been determined by the National Park Service to be strenuous, and we listened as the ranger discussed the 32-foot ladder we

---

1. The mission of the national park is to protect the cultural heritage of twenty-seven Pueblos and Tribes and offer visitors a window into the past. The park contains nearly 5,000 known archeological sites, including cliff dwellings and the mesa top sites of pithouses, pueblos, masonry towers, and farming structures. I wanted to see it *all*. "Mesa Verde National Park (U.S." n.d. National Park Service. Accessed June 27, 2024. https://www.nps.gov/meve/index.htm.

would be climbing and the narrow tunnels we would have to crawl through to get from one point to the next (one of them 12 feet long and the narrowest point being 18 inches). We gathered our water bottles, my backpack, and my camera, and then followed the ranger and our group down a set of stairs that took us to the ladder to the first room.

I spent much of our time at the Balcony House marveling at the up-close view of 800-year-old craftsmanship. The indigenous people who occupied the area had created an engineering masterpiece, but we had to get up close to see it ourselves. The dry climate perfectly preserved the functional wood beams holding some structures together. Bricks were made to fit, with walls reaching to the cathedral-height natural ceiling. The dwellings went back further than the naked eye could see, and the builders engineered methods to heat and cool individual homes. All this, and they discovered methods to deliver enough potable water for all tribal members to have access for drinking, household use, *and* farming.

After a picnic lunch, we met up with our group for what would be the highlight of our Mesa Verde visit: Cliff Palace.

I entered the Cliff Palace tour believing I had seen some of the best Mesa Verde had to offer. After all, we had seen the engineering genius of ancient American peoples and climbed out to spectacular canyon views. But our tour guide promised us that this was his favorite tour, so I descended down the CCC-constructed path expectant but unsure. I climbed the first short ladder. I slowly followed the tour group along rocky paths and cliff faces.

Then I rounded the corner.

I wasn't the only one who let out a tiny gasp as we got our first glimpse of the cliff dwelling with 150 different rooms. It was massive and nearly perfectly preserved. This wasn't a tiny village dwelling—it was an entire town built into a cliff. Our ranger tour guide, ever respectful of the history of the ancestors of the local indigenous tribes, pointed out just how much the ancient people who built the dwellings used their natural surroundings to their fullest. That ancient builders had created such a high standard of living in the rough, high desert mountain climate seemed nothing short of a miracle.

While the trip to Cliff Palace had been fairly easy, the climb out was nearly straight up, first on a short ladder and then on a narrow, steep set of stone stairs that slowly took us back to the parking lot on top. While we had only walked a quarter of a mile, it felt like I had run a full mile by the time we got to the top, the climb and the altitude working against me.

We wrapped up our day driving around the Mesa Top Loop, the gas gauge creeping toward empty as we stopped at archeological sites along the way. We drove to the Chapin Mesa Archeological Museum where the kids could finish their Junior Ranger books and we could stamp our passport books. Our kids earned their third Junior Ranger badge of the trip, getting sworn in at an actual Junior Ranger station in the courtyard, our Cliff Palace ranger tour guide doing the honors.

Our fuel gauge warned we were dangerously low, but when Jeff saw the sign for the Park Point Overlook, he pulled off. Despite the risk, he gave into my love for mountains. Park Point is the highest point in the park and I could finally take pictures of everything: the mountains, cliffs, and valleys in between.

In the end, Mesa Verde was everything I had dreamed about and more. Pictures don't do the dwellings or the landscape justice.

We had several options for the next day, but chose to take it easy. After attending a Hopi rain dance demonstration at the Mesa Verde Visitor Center, I told Jeff I wanted to try to find Yucca House, an obscure national monument.

I had been warned by the ranger working the information desk the first night we arrived in Cortez. When I mentioned wanting to see Yucca House she said, "Just to warn you, it's a little awkward. It is there, but you will have to drive past a person's house to get there." She highly recommended we go to Hovenweep National Monument instead. But we didn't have time for Hovenweep and Yucca House was significantly closer.

Awkward might have been a slight understatement. Our first detour from the main road was accompanied by a sign next to the road saying, "No Trespassing."

"Mom, are you sure we aren't going to get arrested?" Lydia asked from the backseat.

Jeff gave me a withering look from the driver's seat. "Sarah, this feels like another Ohio situation." Once again, he recalled the first time I sent us on a failed stamp quest.

"Honestly, I don't know." I was rethinking the whole idea.

The road ended at a house that was clearly privately owned, so we chose to turn around. After reading the Trip Advisor reviews (an average 3.5 rating), we were not the only ones. According to one traveler blog, there are only about 300 visitors who attempt to find it each year.[2] Those who do find it discover some stunning ruins, but I don't regret leaving. We believe in supporting our national parks, but we draw the line at crossing personal property.

Instead, we ended our Mesa Verde adventures at the campground, recovering before we continued our trip west.

---

2. "Exploring Off-the-Beaten-Path Yucca House National Monument." 2019. Family Well Traveled. https://familywelltraveled.com/2019/03/09/exploring-off-the-beaten-path-yucca-house-national-monument/.

Chapter 29
Arches, Canyons, and Starry Skies

FOR YEARS I HAD been drawn to the pictures of red rocks, natural arches carved out of canyons, and mountains in the distance. They were rugged and majestic, towering over visitors and offering stunning views of the desert landscape to those who braved the hiking trails. I had wanted to see it in person since I was a teenager and I was finally getting my chance.

To make this particular stop even better, Jeff's sister Kristen drove down from Denver to join us for the adventures.

When we finally pulled into the Moab KOA, the kids were eager to see their favorite aunt and try out the campground's inviting pool. We were enjoying the dry desert air, but it was still hot, and we already missed our pool at home. After a quick swim with the family and a quiet drive alone to the Arches National Park Visitor Center so I could pick up maps and Junior Ranger books before they closed, I was ready to plan our next national park adventure.

I woke up early and impatiently waited for my family to be up and ready to go. I had read the park information the night before. If we wanted to get any hiking in, we were on a limited-time budget before the heat of the day got to be too much for us.

We drove through the entire park to get to the Devil's Garden Trailhead, with plans to work back toward the park entrance when we finished the first hike. There was so much to see as we drove to the trailhead and such a contrast: desert, multicolored rocks, and mountains merged together into stunning landscapes. Lydia and Ethan jabbered in the backseat, inventing stories about each new arch and rock formation Jeff drove past.

We arrived at a full parking lot of hikers who had wisely headed out before 11 AM. We convinced ourselves we could handle the heat. After all, I still ran at least three days a week at home. For over a week, Jeff and I had been bragging we could handle the desert heat because it was better than the humidity we had left behind in Houston.

But that was before we arrived in Moab.

We had been warned. There are signs everywhere telling visitors to drink plenty of water and reminding hikers of the dangers of overexposure. By the time we hit the trail, we were nearing the eleven-to-three window that all the tour guides said to avoid. We started on the Landscape Arch trail, less than a mile to where the trail branches off into longer and more difficult trails. Red and tan rocks towered over us as our shoes kicked up the dust beneath our feet. The hike took us to a higher point where we could see spires and arches in the distance, formed by millions of years of water and wind. And yet we all struggled.

There was little shade and the sun beat down on us from a nearly cloudless sky. Ethan, who is used to leading the charge, complained of being warm and said his foot hurt from when he fell while playing catch with a football the day before. By the time we reached the perfect picture spot for the arch at the end of the trail, we were all ready to return to the parking lot. A few short trail detours later, we had hiked nearly two and a half miles with the dry heat creeping close to 100 degrees. It was time for a break.

As we drove back toward the visitor center, we made a detour to Wolfe Ranch to take a picture of Delicate Arch. I gazed longingly at the famous arch, the one pictured prominently on the Utah license plate. One of my dreams for visiting Arches had been hiking up to the landmark, but it was three miles round trip. The rest of my crew was hot and tired and I knew I couldn't and shouldn't do the hike myself. I settled for looking at it from the Upper Viewpoint and zoomed in with my camera. It was the closest I was going to get on this vacation.

When we returned to the KOA, the campground pool called to all of us, answering our need to cool our bodies and eliminate the dust and sweat from our morning hikes. But by the time dinner rolled around, I was anxious to return to the park for sunset to hike up to Windows—a series of arches creating natural windows to the desert landscape beyond—before we ran out of natural light.

But no one else seemed eager to leave. Jeff could see my growing irritation. He scarfed down his sandwich and then said, "Grab my socks and boots. We're leaving."

Thankful for the willing babysitters who had briefly joined us for part of our vacation, we left our happy children with Kristen and her husband and took off. With the sun going down, the 90-degree temperatures were downright pleasant, and we rolled down our windows to take in the growing shadows transforming the entire appearance of the national park.

We again arrived at a packed parking lot of fellow visitors also trying to take in the arches as the sun went down. We climbed the North Window, making it just in time to enjoy the view before watching the sunset over the Double Arch on the other side of the parking lot. The sky turned pink, orange, purple, and blue behind the red rocks and dirt, then gave way to stars slowly revealing themselves in the clear night sky. And I got to experience it with my adventuring partner at my side.

The next day we drove to Canyonlands National Park, thanks to the suggestion of a college friend who offered her advice when I put out a general question on Facebook.[1] We quickly learned that making Canyonlands an "add-on" in my trip planning put us in good company with most national park visitors.

---

1. I had never heard of Canyonlands, even though it is within easy driving distance from Moab. Arches, which is geographically smaller than Canyonlands, gets all of the glory; few people outside of the region make Canyonlands their preferred destination when they visit the parks around Moab. Statistically, Arches sees a staggering one million visitors a year; Canyonlands, only 35 miles away, sees 400,000.

I had a hard time getting the family moving the morning after our second late night in Moab, but I still managed to get us all out of the campground by mid-morning. Lydia and Ethan got sworn in as Junior Rangers at the Arches Visitor Center and then we continued on the road toward the Canyonlands' Island in the Sky Visitor Center.

But it quickly became clear something was off. Ethan, who is usually up for exploring and for years got excited about earning more badges, was sulky and quick with the attitude. When we got to Canyonlands and Lydia and Ethan started working on their Junior Ranger books, he almost fell apart while he and our daughter used a map of the park to answer several questions. Our little problem solver argued map reading was too hard for him and he just wanted to quit. We thought a change of scenery would help, so we all walked to the overlook across the road, but his mood didn't change. Our son was nearing an early meltdown and Jeff and I helplessly looked at each other. If we were going to make the most of the day, we had to stay in the park, but could we do that with a little boy who was falling apart?

Jeff removed him from the group and sat down with him on the edge of the overlook. Ethan lamented the injustice of his sister getting the hiking stick he wanted. Then, he accused me of wanting to do too much, something Jeff consistently reminded me of as I tried to have my family do all of the things. We had been going nonstop for almost a week by this point. Our seven-year-old had hiked and climbed and stayed up late, only to be awakened for more adventuring the following morning. Maybe I was trying to do too much on the vacation, but I had rationalized the packed schedule by telling myself we couldn't just stop after driving so far.

Jeff calmed him down enough to get into the truck and we continued on our way, climbing in elevation. Within minutes, Ethan was sobbing. "My ear!"

Suddenly everything made sense. He had several ear infections as a toddler and difficulties with his ears have always had an impact on his mood.[2] This time, the frequent changes in altitude over the course of our vacation were wreaking havoc on his eardrums and the pressure had finally popped. We rushed to get him Ibuprofen, then made sure he had water to rehydrate from the desert elevation. I frantically worked to comfort my hurting son, feeling guilty I had not figured out what was wrong sooner.

By the time we reached the Mesa Arch parking lot, he was in a completely different mood.

The Mesa Arch hike is only a half-mile round trip, but it is rocky and requires some climbing. The large arch frames the canyon below, terraces and towers expanding to the horizon, displaying the reason for the national park's name. When we all returned to the truck, everyone was in a positive mood and ready to explore just a little more of the Island in the Sky region.[3]

The Canyonlands were considerably more comfortable, the extra 2,000 feet in elevation dropping the temperature down to the high 80s from the high 90s we had experienced the day before. It made the mile round trip hike to the first Upheaval Dome overlook doable. This time, Lydia struggled as we got to the top of the rocky climb, stopping in a small sliver of shade to work on her Junior Ranger book. She turned to the page instructing her to make friends with a rock, picking up a small rock from the trail and holding it in her fist.

I left her for a few minutes to see how Jeff and Ethan were doing and discovered them contentedly working while sitting in a crater at the top of the overlook. Lydia finally joined us at the top so she could work with her brother on their books, telling all of us about

---

2. We had been one more ear infection away from getting tubes, but a final round of antibiotics cleared his ears for a full year. Still, they continued to bother him from time to time as he grew out of toddlerhood.

3. There are three different areas in Canyonlands, Island in the Sky being the closest to Moab. Our goal was to see as much as we could reasonably see in a couple of hours, aware that we had expended a significant amount of energy the day before with the hikes in Arches.

her new rock friend and the stories she had invented while resting under her small shade tree. Jeff and I sat on the flat canyon overlook, glancing back and forth between the deep canyon in front of us and our children diligently helping each other with their tasks. He finally looked at me and said, "We should probably head back." I sighed as I stood up to convince our kids to leave their natural workspace so we could return to Moab.

But Jeff wasn't quite finished with our Canyonlands adventure. Over the course of the vacation, I had gotten to see caves and cliff dwellings and colorful sunsets over the desert landscape. Now it was Jeff's turn to fulfill his own dreams on our way back to Moab, taking the road less traveled down into the canyon instead of on top of it.

Kristen, however, was ready to head back to Moab. Lydia wanted to have her aunt all to herself, so we traded one child for a teenager.

Fifteen years before, when we had joined Kristen in Douglas, Wyoming, on our way home from Yellowstone, Kristen had brought her friend's little girl with her for our single night at the Douglas KOA. That little girl had grown into a high school student living with my sister-in-law in Colorado for the summer. The day before, Kalea proved her worthiness to our son when she voluntarily played football with him. This time, in Canyonlands, we offered her the chance to have an off-road adventure, allowing Lydia the opportunity to return to town with her aunt and uncle. Kalea jumped at the chance to ride back with us.

I had my reservations about the entire excursion. I wasn't ready to take risks with our truck—we needed it to get home. But Jeff was confident in both his truck's capabilities and his driving skills. And I trusted him just enough to go along for the ride.

The road started simple enough, but the gravel country road then made one turn after another, lowering in elevation before finally dropping into the canyon. The road was rough, the decline steep, and then we reached Pucker Pass.

Jeff had shown me a video of the trail, particularly Pucker Pass, with people driving through the seemingly impassible gap in the rocks only to prove there was plenty of room to get through once vehicles were right underneath the rock leaning up against the canyon wall. But the approach is terrifying, especially for someone who is risk averse like me. Everything up to our passage through Pucker Pass had me gripping the handle on the door next to me and wondering why I ever let Jeff talk me into it in the first place, while Ethan and Kalea were in the backseat having the time of their lives.

When we finally reached the bottom, tall, red canyon walls reached up into the blue sky, with small arches carved into the rock faces.

As we emerged from the canyon, we traveled along the Colorado River on our right with the red canyon walls towering over us on our left. We stopped at perfectly preserved petroglyphs high on the rocks overlooking the highway and then parked further down the road for a close-up of the river, so swollen we could see signs underwater. Relieved we had made it out of the canyon alive, I could look back and say it was worth it, even if my hands ached from gripping my door handle for over an hour.

We ended our trip to Arches with a family sunset excursion to the Windows. Lydia, always the climber, scrambled over the rocks to get as high as she could, joined by Kalea who watched out for her when we no longer could reach her. We laid out blankets and watched the sunset beneath the evening clouds, and then observed the slow appearance of stars as the western sky slowly faded to black. Ethan pointed out a small number of bats flying out of the rocks behind us and watched until he couldn't see them anymore.

As Jeff and I snuggled with Ethan on a blanket, he looked up at the stars and then at us. "Can we stay just one more day?"

A day that had started with a meltdown couldn't have ended better. It was a feeling we all wanted to hold onto.

Chapter 30
"There isn't a wheel to put a tire onto"

Our drive from Moab to Albuquerque was already going to be a long day. I had been a willing driver for years, Jeff and I switching off as we traveled everywhere from Yellowstone to Orlando, but once he convinced me we should buy a camper, I was out. I had no interest in driving while towing. It terrified me. The thought of being responsible for my family's safety while pulling an extra 30 feet behind the truck was too much for me.

So Jeff was on his own. At the time, Jeff's ideal for a driving day was about 300 miles, maybe a little more. Even with a heavier-duty hitch, he didn't feel comfortable going over 60 miles per hour while towing. We were going to be pushing it at just over 360 miles for the day. This was after several long days of hiking and late nights, and we were a tired crew. All things considered, the travel day was going pretty well, until Ethan insisted for the second time during the trip that he had to go to the bathroom. With nothing around for miles, Jeff decided to pull over so our son could use the bathroom in the camper. When I pulled myself into the doorway to check on our son, something seemed off. I wasn't sure what it was, but I thought I smelled something burning. However, it was hot, sunny, and I didn't see smoke or heat coming off of anything but the pavement. Besides, the camper had absorbed the outdoor heat and it was possible the stench could have just been a result of the camper being used as a restroom twice while on the road. I decided I would take a closer look at the toilet when we got to Albuquerque.

With less than 50 miles to the KOA, we heard a sudden thud. Jeff looked in his side mirror, exclaiming "Shit!" under his breath as he pulled onto the shoulder. We were in the middle of the desert in New Mexico with no apparent town or city anywhere close.

Jeff got out and investigated. From the backseat, Ethan asked, "Did Daddy say a bad word?"

I tried to mask the worry in my voice as I responded, "Probably. But don't worry about that right now!"

When Jeff got back, I knew it couldn't be good news. "The wheel is gone, and it tore up the side of the slideout."

"What?! Kids, stay here," I admonished before getting out of the truck. Jeff's words didn't make sense. I rushed over to the other side of the truck to see what Jeff was talking about. Now it was my turn. "Shit," I said as I looked at the mangled axle in front of me. Sure enough, we weren't just missing a tire; we were missing an entire wheel.[1] Jeff took off down the shoulder, swearing as he looked for the missing wheel. I tried to swallow the rising panic, looking for the phone number for the roadside assistance we had paid extra for when we purchased the camper less than a year before.

Jeff found the wheel with the popped but intact tire attached nearly half a mile down the road. A highway patrolman stopped to see what kind of help we needed and left Jeff his information. As I prayed for my family's safety on the side of the road, a couple came up and helped Jeff bring the heavy wheel and tire back to our camper.

Then we had to deal with roadside assistance.

Our insurance company said that because it wasn't a tire blowout and was instead a lost wheel with additional damage, it was considered an accident. We would have to pay for the tow and they couldn't give us a solid estimate for how much it would cost. The roadside assistance we paid for was just about as helpful as our insurance company.

---

1. We eventually discovered that the axle had frozen, which caused the chain reaction leading to the wheel exploding off of the camper.

Jeff and I took turns making phone calls, both of us pacing past each other as the New Mexico sun beat down on us. Our multiple shared conversations with operators trying to help us on the Fourth of July went something like this:

"Are you in a safe location?"

"Yes."

"Can you tell us what happened?"

After long explanations, we were consistently told, "We can get a tire repair out to you."

Taking a deep breath: "A tire repair won't help. *There isn't a wheel to put the tire onto.*"

"Where are you located? You will have to pay for the tow, but we don't know exactly how much."

"Really?! I thought roadside assistance was for this very situation!"

And then there was the drama of determining where we were without signs right near us. We found the atlas in the truck and tried to explain where we were, just south of the Zia Indian Reservation, and near Zia Pueblo, but the person on the other end couldn't find it anywhere on the map.

Two hours after the initial incident, Jeff decided we could still make it to town and we would deal with it from there. Despite being down an entire wheel, we were somehow still upright, something we have never stopped being thankful for. He figured that if he drove slowly and avoided the highways we could make it to the KOA in one piece. It was better than waiting for several more hours on the side of the road while two different insurance companies failed to assist us.

We pulled into the campground late but still intact. We used a separate jack in place of the stab jack but we were still seriously off-level, feeling like we were walking through a carnival fun house every time we stepped into the camper. We eventually remedied the situation by getting a second jack to prop up the axle on our second day in Albuquerque, leveling us out some and providing more stability for the six bodies moving around inside.

Suddenly, what was supposed to be a one-night stay turned into an unplanned four-day mini-vacation.

We went to the movie theater and played mini-golf at the KOA. Jeff and I dragged our kids to the Los Pollos Hermanos filming location for *Breaking Bad* and visited the Old Town Plaza, which reminded us a lot of Santa Fe, the adobe structures, tile roofs, and local artisans lifting our dejected spirits.[2] We hiked at Petroglyphs National Monument and I took the kids to Explora, the hands-on children's museum in town; Jeff tried to return to remote work while fielding phone calls about our possible repair.

And then we left our camper in Albuquerque and headed home. We wouldn't see it again for over a month, and while the nearly perfect family vacation had a far-from-perfect ending, we never regretted taking the trip. It was the stuff good family stories were made of, and I was so thankful for how our travel trailer helped us afford such an adventure.

---

2. Interestingly, the filming location of Los Pollos Hermanos is a restaurant called Twisters, a local burger and burrito chain of restaurants in the Albuquerque region.

Chapter 31
"Paddle out of the water, now!"

WHEN WE LEFT OUR camper in Albuquerque, it felt like we left a piece of ourselves behind. We knew we would get it back eventually and theoretically it would be in good condition, but the unknown put a minor halt to our planning for the rest of the year, although I still optimistically planned for both Thanksgiving and Christmas break.

Thankfully, one month after we returned to Houston, the camper dealership in Albuquerque graciously transported the camper to us and we planned a short trip to Sea Rim State Park for the weekend after Labor Day, before soccer schedules would have us locked in for the next two months.[1]

We needed it. Labor Day as a teacher always felt like squeezing two weeks into one. Even the above-average temperatures creeping close to 100 degrees wasn't enough to scare me away. I left as soon as possible on Friday afternoon, picked up the kids, and we rushed home to help Jeff finish loading up the camper. We knew there was no way we would beat the afternoon traffic heading east on I-10, but we did our best.

We arrived at Sea Rim State Park right before sunset, giving us just enough light to park the camper with relative ease. A week earlier Jeff had finally decided it was time to improve our camping communication and purchased a set of radios so we could talk without yelling.

---

1. We agreed to let the rest of the reimbursements for extra lodging and service calls go.

For the first time in six years of camping with an RV, I didn't stress about telling Jeff where we were going and what he needed to do. I could just talk to him through the radio and he could talk back to me when he didn't understand. We wondered why it took us so long to find a solution.

The emerging mosquitoes rushed our set-up routine, the kids and dogs sent inside as we finished unhooking and connecting electricity and water. Then, as I was trying to get water into the icemaker and the filter pitcher, I noticed a drop in our water pressure. Eventually, there was no water at all.[2]

An investigation of the other campsites revealed that no one in the campground had water. I freaked out.

I was already a little skittish because I had nearly stepped on the same snake twice.[3] And with no water, I had to make a sudden change to dinner plans. Jeff was already cooking the steak, but without water, rice was clearly out as a side dish. I pulled out the baked beans and corn and started cooking them on our outdoor stove. While dinner was good and we had beverages for the time being, the complete loss of water had me more than a little rattled. Without water, we had no way to take care of the dogs, we couldn't do dishes, and we couldn't brush teeth or clean hands and faces. In the past, we had brought bottled water with us in case the water was no good, but with the water being filtered through the hose and then again through our Brita pitcher, we had moved away from buying bottled water in an effort to be more eco-friendly.

---

2. Most RV sites in Texas state parks have water available at the site. It had been a long time since we had been required to fill our tank with water and I wasn't used to not having water on demand.

3. I love the outdoors, but I have an Indiana Jones-like aversion to snakes. And while there was always a possibility we would encounter venomous snakes in Indiana, the number and variety in Texas increased our odds. I looked it up when we got home and it appears that I had a close encounter with the Gulf Coast Ribbon Snake, which is safe to humans.

Unfortunately, this would have been the time to have the wasteful bottles along.

I panicked. This was our first time out since we had been stuck in Albuquerque. This was our chance to relax before the next two months of weekends full of soccer games and grading. All I wanted was a relaxing weekend away with my family so we could prove to ourselves that the end to our summer vacation hadn't derailed our love for camping and exploring state parks. Fresh drinking water was an essential part of our ability to stay and I didn't want the uncertainty to ruin our entire weekend.

I kept going back and forth between our indoor faucets and the water spigot outside, looking around our campsite to see if there was any other water supply I could try. Unlike most Texas State Parks, Sea Rim was bare bones, the only restroom facility pit toilets on the way to the beach. Jeff, watching my growing anxiety, finally grabbed my arms and looked me in the eye. "Sarah, there is nothing we can do about it right now. Settle down. We'll figure it out in the morning."

After the kids were settled in for the night, I eventually buried myself in our bed, resigning myself to reading a book I was now determined to finish before we got home. It gave me a goal to distract me from our current situation. Somehow, I fell asleep, even with the uncertainty of the following morning.

I woke up and turned the water on in the kitchen. It worked. I quickly filled the fresh water tank, just to be safe.

Then Ethan woke up simply happy to be alive. "Mommy, thank you for letting us stay here and camp in our camper." He was camping, he would get to explore during the day, and his precious Michigan Wolverines were going to be playing in a couple of hours and we had enough reception for him to watch the game.

He was completely settled in his happy place.

Eventually, the entire family was awake and fed. With an hour to spare before the Michigan game would start, we walked down the boardwalk to the beach, promising the kids we could return once we were done watching the Michigan game.

Our Albuquerque misadventures had reminded me of Jeff's initial purpose in buying the Roo all those years ago: time away as a family. And while we had prioritized unplugging from the internet and devices as an important part of getting away, I gradually learned I needed to be more flexible with the changing desires and interests of our growing kids. I also needed to adjust my expectations relative to the elements. For the first time since I had caved to Jeff watching bowl games on our frozen anniversary in the Davis Mountains, we turned on the TV for college football.

We spent the heat of the midday inside watching a football game, and then I gave in to Jeff's desires and we rented two-person kayaks for our family, a kid accompanying each parent.

We enjoyed a late afternoon row on the easy trail, less than a mile leading to a small body of still water close to Fence Lake. The first half of the trip was mostly uneventful. Lydia tried to help me, but my need for control had me frequently telling her to get the paddle out of the water whenever we got close to vegetation on either bank. I wasn't just worried about getting stuck or tipping over. The ranger who rented us the gear had told us to be on the lookout for alligators. The last thing I wanted to do was accidentally push off of a gator's head or fall on top of one that might be swimming underneath our kayak. Our years camping in Huntsville and a day trip to hike Brazos Bend State Park southeast of Houston had taught me alligators were not prone to unprovoked attacks on humans. But I didn't want to invade their territory and make my daughter or myself an easy target by splashing into the marsh.

The kayak path split, one side taking adventurers toward more water trails and a floating campsite, the other leading to a small lake we could circle for our return to the docks. I considered turning around where we were. The path to the prescribed turnaround was narrow, but Jeff yelled at me from ahead, "Sarah, keep coming. You need to see this." So against my better judgment, we continued on.

We were nearly out into open water when my heart stopped. I glanced down as our daughter pulled her oar out of the water, lifting it high and swinging it over the water's surface. Two glassy eyes peered at me from where her paddle had just swung and slowly sank back into the murky water.

"Paddle out of the water, now!" I hissed.

"Every time I put the paddle in the water you tell me to get it back out!" she argued, convinced I was telling her that she wasn't capable of helping with the kayak. And yes, I had been a bit controlling and critical about her paddling technique, directing her every move as we glided through the water. But I wasn't going to tell her she had been inches away from hitting an alligator on the head. That news could wait for once we were safely back onshore.

My heart thumping, we caught up with Jeff and our son, rowing into the marsh right next to Fence Lake. He was right, it was lovely, but I couldn't stop thinking about the gator I knew was hanging out in the general area.

Jeff smoothly navigated his way out of the turnaround and worked his way ahead of us. My transition out was not quite so smooth. I rowed our kayak right into a patch of shallow weeds, digging deep with my paddle to get back into deeper water so we could get out of there. Frantic to get away from the alligator I was sure lurked nearby, I became less efficient by the minute. By the time I finally had the kayak free, I had covered Lydia and me in thick, pungent mud from the bottom of the marsh. Jeff hadn't heard me yelling for help and when we finally got to them, he was ready to give me the lead. I knew better. Letting him and Ethan go ahead was going to be better for everyone.

When we finally returned to the shore, I was exhausted and covered in drying mud. But despite the gator scare, I was glad we had taken the family trip on the water.

We arrived back at the front gate to the campground and beach to discover a boil water advisory. If we wanted safe drinking water, we would have to boil and cool it first. Apparently, the water main break from the night before eventually caused concerns about water safety.

Jeff looked at me, "What do you want to do?"

I sighed. "If we stay one more night, one of us has to run into town to get water bottles for drinking. I don't really want to do that when we only have to travel an hour and a half to go home."

"Then we'll all change and give the kids time to play in the water. It's the last thing we wanted to do anyway, right?" Jeff said as he directed the kids back into the camper to get into their swimming suits.

We all walked out into the bathwater-warm Gulf of Mexico, and I rinsed my mud-caked legs as the waves splashed up my thighs. Both kids walked out 15 to 20 yards, the water still just hitting their knees. They jumped waves while we discussed our options. We had done everything we planned to do while at the state park and with the abundance of nighttime mosquitoes coming out of the marsh, we knew we would be spending most of the night inside.

It was decided; after the kids got a little more time playing in the water and collected their seashells from the wide-open beach, we were heading home.

The weekend didn't go quite as planned, but honestly, that's okay. We discovered a pretty and simple, albeit rustic, state park perfect for those who want beach time and water activities without the crowds. We got some much-needed quality family time and the fresh air we had all been craving.

My family was getting used to rolling with the camping punches. We didn't need it to be perfect every time.

Chapter 32

"I had to protect the sea turtles"

WE STARTED PLANNING OUR next Campsgiving as we traveled home from our time in Louisiana with Jeff's family. Three years in a row of camping for Thanksgiving had fully convinced us that camping was the only way to properly do Thanksgiving, and we knew we had to book early if we wanted to get our ideal location.

We tossed around options, looked at past camping trips around Texas, and six months out finally decided to give the Corpus Christi region another shot. At the time, Mustang Island State Park was still closed for repairs from Hurricane Harvey, so I looked a little further north to Lake Corpus Christi State Park. It would be less than an hour of driving to get us into the city for whatever sightseeing we wanted to do and, as a bonus, we could get a full hook-up, which meant we could dump our wastewater at our campsite.

The drive down the coast was far from smooth. The wind cut across farmland, bending trees and straightening flags all while wearing down Jeff's nerves. Once again, I was both thankful for my husband's willingness to drive our family to fulfill my whims and scared about the prospect of ever being the one behind the wheel. Thankfully, even with a lunch stop at Buc-ee's and a detour around traffic, we arrived at Lake Corpus Christi before dark.[1]

---

1. Buc-ee's is a chain of super gas stations that started in the Houston area and has now spread across the southwest. Think Cracker Barrel storefront plus a truck stop with parking for hundreds of cars and trucks.

It looked like getting set up was going to be a breeze, until we pulled into our campsite. We've had a mix of easy and difficult campsites over the years, but we've only rarely had to deal with barriers that complicate what should be an easy parking job. The previous summer in Monahans Sandhills State Park we had to deal with a metal pole preventing us from opening up the main slide out, leading to multiple attempts at finding the right parking position. This time we were dealing with a wooden pole in the same unfortunate spot.

With walkie-talkies in hand, we tried to engineer the best possible parking situation. Finally, I got my aerobic workout for the night as I kept moving blocks so we could eventually park far enough away from the pole to enable us to put our slide out. We would spend the next three nights parked with one side of the camper on the concrete slab and the other half on top of yellow one-inch blocks.

I eagerly woke up the next morning to make a traditional camping breakfast. After setting the food and dishes on the picnic table I looked into the grove of trees behind our campsite and told Jeff to look into the clearing. He looked at me and said, "You know, that would be a perfect place for a tent." He helped the kids find the small two-person tent he had bought on super clearance on a business trip and they begged us to let them sleep in it that night. While Jeff and I finished breakfast dishes, they spent the pre-exploring time carrying their toys, blankets, and pillows from the camper to the tent.

"We're going to have a sleepover with nature," Ethan announced.

Jeff and I laughed. Then we loaded up the truck to explore near Corpus Christi.

Lydia's love for animals had grown over the years. While she had always cared for her dogs, when we moved to Texas she went through a cat phase, our insistence that Jeff was allergic to cats being the only guard against her picking up a stray cat and begging us to keep it. For a time, the more she learned about animals and the environment, the more she wanted to work in a zoo and with animal rescue. As I was planning our short trip, I discovered the Texas Sealife Center, an animal rescue near Padre Island. When I asked Lydia if she wanted to go to a sea life animal rescue, she was convinced that meant she was going to personally go out into the Gulf and rescue animals and she eagerly said yes.

Unfortunately, she learned when we arrived that she was only going to see animals that had already been rescued.

As we entered the center, we saw cages and small pools housing snakes, lizards, and exotic birds. The reptiles were either illegal in Corpus or too domesticated to live on their own. The birds were injured to the point of being unable to take flight. We even saw an angry-looking opossum awaiting veterinarian care from behind wire mesh.

But the highlight was the sea turtles being treated for fibropapillomatosis so they could eventually be released back into the wild.[2] Well, most of them could be released. One of the turtles had been a victim of both a shark attack and then a run-in with a boat, so it was a permanent resident. But it was exciting to see the sea turtles up close, knowing eventually they would be back in their home in the Gulf of Mexico. It was a great learning experience for all, made our dreaming daughter happy, and was well worth the $20 donation we had to make as a family to get the tour.

Fifteen minutes after leaving the center, we arrived at Padre Island National Seashore. The first time we had been there in November, it had been balmy, gentle waves kissing our ankles as we explored the shoreline. This time the cold wind whipped up both sand and surf. The kids did as much of their Junior Ranger books as they possibly could inside the visitor center, and then we took their trash bags outside so they could collect trash for their final Junior Ranger task. They were semi-successful, but we gave up long before they got close to filling their bags. I couldn't keep sand or my hair out of my eyes and we were done with walking along the beach.

---

2. Fibropapillomatosis is a disease that causes internal and external tumors in sea turtles. They aren't necessarily fatal, but they can cause issues that make life in the wild difficult.

Despite the forecasted coastal flooding and rising tide, Jeff decided we should drive at least part of the way on the coastal trail that allowed for off-roading right on the beach. Suddenly, we heard "Stop!" coming from the backseat, and then a door opening from our slowly moving vehicle. Lydia jumped out as Jeff stopped and we looked at each other, both of us trying to figure out what had happened as we prepared to join our daughter on the beach. Lydia returned to the truck, proudly grasping a tangled mess of fishing wire. "I had to get this off the beach to protect the sea turtles." We still don't know how she saw the clear fishing line from her truck window, but she had been observant enough for just the moment.

As much as I wanted to help her clean the beach and save more animals, we didn't have a way to collect all of the coastal junk. With the clump sitting in her hands, Lydia could feel she had protected at least one animal from digesting a deadly clump of sea trash, and that satisfied her enough.

When we finally made it back to the campground, we had just enough time for the kids and Jeff to go fishing while I made dinner. I got the potatoes started on the grill and then joined my family for a couple of minutes of togetherness before I headed back to the campsite to finish dinner. I may not have wanted to fish, but the light on the dock allowed me to get some pleasure reading done while everyone else happily baited hooks and cast lines into the water.

Immediately following dinner, the kids headed straight out to the tent, where they were determined to spend the entire night. This would be Ethan's first experience sleeping in a tent overnight and Lydia's first night she would remember.

Much to our delight, they made it until morning.

Our low-key Thanksgiving included traditional dinner, a drive around the park to enjoy the CCC architecture, and each of us taking time to breathe and slow down in our own way. The kids also decided to spend their last night in the camper because the rough ground had lost its novelty. Jeff and I couldn't help but smile at their revelation.

After spending the two previous Thanksgivings with extended family, we once again enjoyed the quiet time away with just the four of us. And we had a lot to be thankful for.

Chapter 33
"Why would we want to ride Jeeps?"

DURING OUR FIRST CHRISTMAS vacation out west, we fell in love with Big Bend National Park, mourning the loss of extra time to explore due to the government shutdown. We vowed we would return, and eventually decided the following Christmas was the right time to do so.

This time we made our halfway stop South Llano River State Park, returning to the park where we started our 2019 summer vacation. The kids begged for a tent night, piling their blankets and pillows and extra sleeping bags into the tent. We weren't sure how long they would last through the steadily dropping temperatures, but it was the only night of our trip this would be a possibility. Ethan, all cozy in my 20-degree mummy sleeping bag, eventually fell asleep while staring at the stars. Lydia, who had covered her brother's face with a stuffed animal to keep his head warm, was still awake as we neared midnight. Unable to fall asleep, she finally caved and decided to sleep inside. Jeff picked up our very sleepy son and carried him to his bed inside so he wouldn't wake up in the tent alone.

We spent the next day traveling another 360 miles, arriving in Terlingua right before dark.

Big Bend is the most remote national park we have ever been to. Even Arches has a fairly large town right outside of it. Terlingua is a "blink and you'll miss it" town, but the RV park we reserved had everything we needed. The kids discovered a pool table in the game room and wanted us to teach them how to play. The dogs got their walks around the campground, and Jeff turned on the hotspot he had brought for work emergencies so we could find out what was happening in the park over the next three days and make our plans.

The year before we had rushed our way through the 800,000-acre park in less than six hours. This time we had three full days. We could take our time and explore.[1]

The first item on *my* vacation bucket list was finally using the passports we had acquired the year before. We had done our research before making our trip to the Big Bend region in 2018. We had our passports. This time, with the border open, we weren't passing up the chance to leave the country for a couple of hours.

We were heading to Mexico.[2]

As we drove to the border crossing, Jeff sheepishly glanced in my direction. "Sarah, I know you love a good hike, but I really think we should rent burros for our trip into Boquillas." I had been hearing this argument for days. He wasn't letting it go.

I signed. "But you hate horses. Isn't riding a donkey kind of the same thing?"

"It's all about the experience, Sarah. Why don't you ask the kids?"

I rolled my eyes as I turned around to the kids. "What do you think? Should we rent burros once we get to Mexico?"

Both kids gave us an emphatic no.

---

1. To give an idea of how much area Big Bend National Park covers, it is twenty miles from the entrance of the park to Panther Junction, the first of five visitor centers in Big Bend. The Big Bend region itself covers hundreds of miles of territory, called so because of the actual bend in the Rio Grande River, the natural border between Texas and Mexico. Technically, our stay in the Davis Mountains during the previous Christmas break had also been in the Big Bend region, and that was 100 miles away from the park.

2. Boquillas Crossing has been an important part of Big Bend National Park history since nearly the beginning. It was never intended to be a free-for-all open border but instead an open partnership between the US and Mexican governments to preserve hundreds of thousands of acres of land on either side of the river and keep the village of Boquillas open for American visitors looking to cross the border.

"Are you sure?"

"Why would we want to ride Jeeps when we get there?"

Our city kids believed that burro meant Jeep, which would have been a very different experience, indeed. Jeff and I laughed.

Shaking my head, I said, "Burros are donkeys. We're asking if you want to ride an animal once we cross the river."

"Oh..." they responded in unison. Ethan nodded in agreement as Lydia said, "Yes. But I thought Dad didn't like horses."

"It's different," Jeff said, although none of us were quite sure *how* it was different, no matter how hard he argued. And Jeff and I have never let the kids forget they once mistook burros for Jeeps.

We paid for the boat ride across the river and, despite my desire to *walk* into Boquillas, rented burros to transport us to the village. Both kids giggled as the beasts of burden slowly jostled them to and fro, occasionally picking up speed when they fell behind. Since there was no one there to check our passports on the Mexico side, we freely explored the village with our burro guide following us along the way. We knew this wasn't the norm for most of the border between the United States and Mexico, but we were thankful for the comfortable relationship between the National Parks Service and our southern neighbors. In a way, it was a throwback to the border relationship over a hundred years before, the constant flow of workers and family members passing back and forth between the United States and Mexico.

During our family's first trip out of the country, we ate at one of the two local restaurants, drank from glass bottles, found a geocache, visited the local church, and let the kids pick out a couple of hand-made souvenirs. For the first time ever, we weren't just showing our children remote parts of their country, we were exposing them to the world. Our camping adventures were taking us out of the country, even if it was brief, and they couldn't wait to tell their friends about it when they returned to school in January.

Despite Jeff's fears that we would get stuck in Mexico, the whole visit took us about two hours.[3] We returned across the border with plenty of time to get through the immigration check-in with our passports and visit other parts of the east side of Big Bend before dark.

I had gotten my wish to travel out of the country; now Jeff wanted to relive our post-Canyonlands adventure by taking an unimproved road to another geocache location. We turned onto Old Ore Road and traveled along the scenic, bumpy, windy four miles to the Ernst Tinaja trail turn-off. The leaves of tall yucca plants scraped against our side mirrors and we had to move over to the side to occasionally allow another vehicle heading the opposite direction to pass us, but thirty minutes after turning onto Old Ore we were hiking down the trail.

It was worth all of the bumps along the way.

We stepped over waves of sandstone, changing in color and texture the closer we got to Ernst Tinaja. When we finally arrived at our destination, both kids took off to climb up the rocks flanking the sides of a series of pools, only one of which was visible from the bottom. We all climbed up to the top and walked about 50 feet further to see additional rock formations unlike any we had ever seen, even in our time around Arches, before deciding to head back since we didn't have the climbing equipment necessary to go further.

We finished our day with a return to the historic Hot Springs. I realized when we were about 30 miles outside of Houston we had forgotten our swimming suits, so once again we would have to pass on jumping into the water. We looked into the historic buildings, put our feet in the riverside pool heated by the hot spring, and walked back on the sandy trail without our shoes, finally putting on our hiking boots when the rocks got to be too much for our bare feet.

We wrapped up the day with a stop at the Panther Junction Visitor Center so the kids could walk the path in front of the building,

---

3. The national park port of entry closes at exactly 5 PM, no exceptions.

answering the questions about plants in their Junior Ranger books. While they raced against the fading sunlight to finish their research, I watched a small family of javelinas cross the path behind the visitor center. It wasn't a bear, but it was more wildlife to add to the coyote and roadrunner we had seen earlier in the day.[4]

The next morning, we headed down Old Maverick Road as soon as we entered the national park. Because it is an unimproved thoroughfare, it is certainly the road less traveled. While it is technically a two-lane drive and significantly less curvy with fewer dramatic climbs and descents than we'd experienced on Old Ore Road, the 25-mile-per-hour speed limit occasionally felt a little generous. We enjoyed the scenic route revealing intimate views of desert landscapes and hidden gems highlighting the long and desolate history of the region.

We eventually turned toward Santa Elena Canyon, the Rio Grande running through it. We followed our fellow park visitors around the flooded creek, taking the treacherous climb up the bank over the packed dirt, rocks, and vegetation, finally landing on a path.

We walked past river vegetation, climbed up stairs and a ramp, and then descended into the canyon, walking along the sandy path past reeds, oversized river plants, and boulders that called to our children, begging to be climbed. Both kids challenged their limits by repeatedly begging to climb another oversized rock, Lydia getting stuck once and needing the help of a stranger because she didn't realize her height didn't match the gap between the two rocks she had chosen for climbing, making it difficult to get down.

When we reached the end of the trail, we stared right into a peaceful canyon, the clear waters of the Rio Grande disappearing into the tall red and black canyon walls, all in the middle of the Texas desert.

The hike had been worth the initial challenge.

---

4. Yes, we did see both in the same day and yes, Jeff and I referenced the *Looney Toons* when it happened, although the kids had no idea what we were talking about.

We left the canyon and drove to the Castolon Visitor Center so the kids could get sworn in for their eighth Junior Ranger badge of 2019. We toured the historic buildings, the teacher mom working too hard to turn another vacation into a learning opportunity.

But the best lesson of the day would come once the sun went down.

Big Bend National Park has been rated the best place in the continental United States to stargaze. With nearly no light pollution from the surrounding area and careful measures taken by the park staff, it has earned its top rating for being a certified dark sky park. By the time we followed the red rope lighting to the parking area behind the visitor center and put down our chairs, we were joined by a sizable crowd of fellow park visitors who also wanted to learn from the rangers.

We listened as the lead ranger discussed constellations, satellites, star systems, and used a super laser pointer to show us where everything was in the night sky.[5] Lydia volunteered to play the part of the sun in a demonstration of the location of planets in our solar system and we all got to look through a telescope to view the craters on the crescent moon. While we were told the program could last up to two hours, we happily returned to the truck just over an hour after our arrival, the desert temperatures dropping into the 40s by the time we started the dark drive home.

Our last day in the park once again coincided with our wedding anniversary, and I wanted to hike.

We had been warned the day before that if we wanted to go to Chisos Basin and be guaranteed parking, we needed to be in the region before 10 AM. Jeff and I spent the night before looking at the maps and determining which hike we wanted to try as a family. After the shorter hike the previous Christmas break, this time we wanted to try to take our eight- and ten-year-old on either the Lost Mine

---

5. Despite numerous tutorials, I *still* fail to see constellations, but it was nice to listen to someone who can identify them for me.

(over five miles) or the Window Trail (just around five miles). We were being ambitious.

Unfortunately, by the time we got into the Chisos Basin region, after nine but well before ten o'clock, the limited parking for the Lost Mine Trail was already taken. When we asked the ranger at the Chisos Basin Visitor Center, her skepticism at our ability to take a hike on the trail seeped through, telling us to come back the next day because we would need to be in the park by seven o'clock if we wanted a parking spot for that hike. Since this was our last day and that was *not* an option for us, we decided we would have to take the Window hike. If we started in the campground instead of at the visitor center, we could cut out nearly a mile round trip from the hike, so we first tried to find parking there and failed. We headed back up the hill, found an empty spot behind the lodge restaurant and gift shop, and started toward the trailheads. We were going to attempt the five-mile hike dangerously close to lunchtime.

The Window Trail spends the first half of the five miles descending into the Basin to see the base of the Window and the second half climbing back up out of the Basin. Ethan had already claimed he was tired after two long days of exploring, but we fed them healthy snacks and then headed out in the deceptive bright sun, prepared for our 34-degree hike.

The kids were troopers, but the cold fingers and tired bodies led to a near meltdown by children and mom alike, mine fueled by the impending kid meltdown. After I had snapped at our son for dropping his hiking stick four times in quick succession, Jeff pulled me aside. "Sarah, Ethan is hungry. Both kids are tired. Maybe it's time to call it quits and head back."

I humbled myself to talk to Ethan and ask him what he wanted to do. The hike was beautiful, but we were over half a mile away from the end of the trail and we would still have to climb out of the basin to return to our truck. "Mom, I don't want to ruin your anniversary. I want you to be happy."

Mommy Sarah took over for Adventurer Sarah. I looked into his eyes. "Honey, you're not ruining our anniversary, I promise. I know you're hungry and tired. We can go back if you want." Relief washed over his face as I swallowed my disappointment and turned my family around to head back up the trail.

It's one of the important lessons travel and outdoor explorations have taught me as a mom. I never regret humbly asking for my kids' forgiveness when I let my desire to do too much trump their needs, even as they change each year and grow bigger and more capable. But like with the tears in Canyonlands National Park, I had to take a moment to listen to the needs of those who depend on me the most.

But not all was lost for the day.

On our way back to the RV park, we stopped in Terlingua Ghost Town.[6]

Following the self-guided tour created by local artisans, we looked down a mine shaft, walked around the decrepit Perry School, stepped inside St. Agnes Church, and temporarily locked the kids in the Terlingua Jail.

Then Jeff pulled out the GPS to see if the family could find one of three geocaches in the area.

What started as one geocache quickly turned into three geocaches, the last one taking us to Long Draw Pizza, a local pizza joint, where we eventually ordered some anniversary dinner to take back to the camper.

---

6. Terlingua Ghost Town is a good example of what happens to a town when a particular industry dries up. At the turn of the 20th century, Terlingua became home to about 2,000 people, thanks to a thriving mercury mine. Workers from both sides of our southern border worked side-by-side to make the mine successful for several years before it finally dried up after World War II. In the 1970s, people slowly started repopulating the area, and while Terlingua is by most measures a "blink and you'll miss it" kind of town, local residents are trying to bring it back. The Ghost Town, which was the business center of the region in the first half of the 20th century, has now become an artist colony.

To be honest, I could spend every Christmas break visiting Big Bend National Park. The rugged beauty of the region offered everything we needed to recharge as a family over two very different winter vacations. But that would be the last time our family would visit, at least for the time being.

Chapter 34
Camping to Escape COVID

WHEN COVID-19 CAME, IT knocked us off of our feet.

I returned from spending almost a week in Costa Rica with a group of students days before the country shut down its border to outside visitors. No one in our house returned to school after spring break. I went to work the week after spring break to receive online teaching instructions, for what was believed to only be a month at most, and within the first week our whole family found personal stations for work and school. Jeff eventually moved his home office out into the garage.

Our family hit an awkward, imperfect rhythm as I managed my children doing their own remote learning while teaching my students from our dining room table. The only people we saw outside of our home were the Mahals as we continued to send our kids back and forth between our houses and discussed the challenges of pandemic parenting. I obsessively checked the news reports for cases in Houston, praying my family wouldn't be exposed. Eventually, Jeff and I started leaving the kids at home so we could run errands and pick up more items for the COVID home improvement projects we devised, using our pent-up energy to make a bed frame, install new stair treads on our staircase, and completely gut and rebuild our family room wet bar.

Despite the distractions, it didn't take long for us to feel trapped, even for the introverts in our home. I just wanted time to myself, and runs in our neighborhood weren't enough. I wanted space and fresh air and our kids wanted to move. Spring soccer disappeared and

Ethan needed to do more than walk next door to visit his best friend. Even our pool failed to be enough to keep us all happy.

We had lost Easter Sunday celebrations at church and hosting Easter dinner for our friends in our home. The kids and I had lost end-of-the-year celebrations to wrap up the school year. The kids missed their friends. I missed my students and colleagues. Jeff and I missed going out for dates and getting away for a few hours dedicated to our relationship instead of parenting. The pandemic felt like it was constantly taking away something else, stripping us of experiences and memories we had come to expect.

The one thing we weren't going to let the pandemic take away from us was our planned summer vacation to Colorado.

When COVID was still a mysterious disease far away from us, before we knew what the future held, we had carefully planned a vacation that would take us up through Colorado so we could explore as many national parks as possible with Kristen. She was going to drive down from Denver and meet us in Colorado Springs, caravanning with us for the remainder of our summer vacation.

And since camping *still* appeared to be the safest way to travel and protect our family, we stuck with the plan. Jeff drove for three days, taking us across Texas and up through central Colorado, just in time to connect with Kristen.

When Jeff and I went to Colorado for our pre-marriage trip, the one that got me into a tent for the next several years, we also spent a day driving through Colorado Springs and the Garden of the Gods. I fell in love with the hiking and red rock formations and the mountains rising in the distance.

In the following years, I looked at others' photographs of the park with envy, longing to see the rock garden again someday.

Going back was always going to be a part of a Colorado family vacation.

In my wildest dreams, I never imagined I would return to the Garden of the Gods during a global pandemic. I never imagined the fears I would hold and the precautions I would make my family take as we finally emerged into public for the first time in nearly three months. Kristen, who ran a youth center in one of the poorest regions of Denver, had been taking even more precautions, following Colorado state laws that were far more restrictive than in Texas. And because she was in the middle of a divorce, she had consistently been around fewer people than we had.

We carried face masks everywhere we went, putting them up and down anytime we got close to another group of explorers. I worried about protecting others from the germs we brought with us from Texas. I worried about catching the germs of others who had also taken a pilgrimage to Colorado, hopeful for a temporary escape from the frightening news cycle. But being out in nature eased some of the tension of the past months. When we finally arrived at the Garden of the Gods, we walked the trails, the kids climbed rocks that matched their size and ambitions, and we all took in the natural beauty. It had been everything I remembered and more.

We breathed a sigh as we once again escaped the crowds of hikers to travel up the road toward Pikes Peak, another Colorado bucket list item I hoped we would still be able to do despite restrictions.

I had only been to Pikes Peak once, when I was sixteen and on a family vacation with my dad's extended family. I remembered the beautiful views and that was pretty much it. All I knew was I wanted to make sure that if our kids were in central Colorado, they got to see the top of the world.

When we got to the gateway of the Pikes Peak Highway, the 19-mile road that leads straight to the top, the ranger warned us the peak had been temporarily closed while a lightning storm lit up the upper regions of the mountain. There was a possibility the road would open up eventually, but he had no way of knowing. We decided to pay the $50 fee for our truckload of five and continue on. Jeff drove up the mountain highway while the rest of us took in the sights of pine trees and distant valleys.

We made our first stop at Mile-7 to take in the views at Crystal Reservoir and eat a really late lunch. [1] Then we continued up the winding road until we got to Glen Cove, hoping we would find the road open so we could continue to the top, or even better, that there would be a shuttle waiting for us so we could travel to the top in comfort.

The closer we got to the Mile-13 stop, the more vehicles we saw coming down the mountain covered in what appeared to be snow. Once we parked, we discovered hail, not snow, littering the ground. While Kristen and I stood in line to find out what was happening with the top (which was blocked when we arrived), the kids and Jeff started having a makeshift snowball fight, using the hail as a substitute.

Since it didn't look like an ascent was going to be possible, we walked around the pine and spruce trees as the kids jumped on rocks. I took pictures of the snow-speckled mountains rising above us. Frustrated by the first big hiccup in my elaborate summer plans, I resigned myself to the real possibility we wouldn't make it to the top.

But then the road opened up just as we were getting ready to head back down the mountain. Instead of turning around, we piled back into the truck and started the climb up.

The drive up was nothing like I remembered. Tight hairpin turns and switchbacks kept us at around 15 miles per hour, the juxtaposition of Jeff's white knuckles and my wide eyes telling the story of what it is like to travel on a road that takes you to 14,000 feet. The breathtaking views contrasted narrow roads and drop-offs that increased our blood pressure.

---

1. At that point, we had already reached 9,160 feet.

And at the top? We were pelted with hail and snow and we all fought the dizziness accompanying the thin air at the top, Lydia suffering the worst of it. As I watched my daughter struggle to maintain equilibrium, I flashed back to the first time Jeff and I had been in the mountains together. Wanting to rescue her from the same fate as her father, I agreed to rush our visit to the top and return to a lower elevation. Besides, thanks to the hail and snow, we couldn't even see the valleys below us, our view blocked by nature herself.

The trip down the mountain was more nerve-wracking than the trip up. Another ranger checked our brakes at Glen Cove. He told us to rest our brakes the next chance we had and so we stopped for a little while before continuing down the mountain to where French dip was waiting for us at our campsite.

And now it was time to continue our drive north.

When my family lived in Wyoming through my junior high and early high school years, we spent every Thanksgiving driving down to Fort Collins, Colorado, to visit my mom's aunts and uncles and cousins who lived in the greater Denver area. Part of that yearly trip included traveling in my great-aunt and great-uncle's motorhome up into the mountains for the yearly post-Thanksgiving Day parade in Estes Park. The trip was always bitterly cold, required multiple layers, and usually included a reward of hot chocolate for making it through the experience without *too* much whining.

But despite our pre-marital camping trip to the region and living so close to Rocky Mountain National Park during the five years I lived in Wyoming with my family, I had never actually been *in* the park. When I made the vacation plans before the genuine threat of COVID-19, I knew we would need two days in the park to do what we wanted to do without overdoing it.

After we arrived in Estes, parked the camper, and set up camp, Kristen and I drove to the entrance to get maps and Junior Ranger books for the kids. It was too late in the day to explore the park, but we stopped at the visitor center and gift shop immediately outside of the park and picked up the books and sticker stamps for our passport books.

With most national parks going through a phased re-opening, we had to accommodate for the restrictions the popular summer destination had put into place, which included a timed entry so they could avoid handling any money or credit cards, limit the number of visitors, and stagger the visitors coming to the park before five o'clock in the evening.

By the time we arrived at the park the following morning, the Bear Lake parking lot was reportedly full, so we parked in the park and ride and took the shuttle to the trailhead at Bear Lake. Colorado had even more restrictions in place than at home in Texas, but we were spending more time around people than we had in months. Kristen and I were admittedly a little nervous about being in a closed space with strangers, but the park officials limited the number of people in each shuttle and repeatedly emphasized the importance of wearing a mask, and I forced my family to comply.

Then we were ready to hit the trails.

We stopped periodically to sip water and take pictures, the kids suddenly enamored by the chipmunks running up and down the trail. We first reached Nymph Lake, half a mile up the trail, and then continued climbing. We were almost to Dream Lake when Ethan announced he was done and ready to head back.

We hadn't seen the second of the three lakes and he hadn't had a chance to play in the snow. We weren't letting him give up that easily.

Thankfully, Aunt Kristen was quick to the rescue. "Here buddy, I have M&Ms. Why don't you have a few and then we can talk about what we're going to do next?" Ethan and Lydia both quickly agreed to the bribe.

A rest and a snack at a waterfall and we were good to go. We came across a large patch of snow right next to the trail and gave our two Texan transplants a chance to relive just a small piece of their early childhood by encouraging them to play in the snow.

Then we continued to Dream Lake, a huge body of mountain water surrounded by snow drifts calling to both of our children. Neither of them wanted to leave the snow, so Kristen agreed to stay back with the kids and play while we continued on to Emerald Lake.

The hike to Emerald Lake was beautiful, full of waterfalls and climbs over snowdrifts covering the path. It was also an unforgivingly straight climb up. We climbed stairs of stone, stairs made with timber beams, and rocky dirt paths going nowhere but up. And we were doing this at an elevation at least 7,000 feet above our normal lives at sea level in Houston, Texas.

It was Jeff who decided, on our last leg of the hike after we had left the kids with Kristen, that this was the "Stairmaster of hikes," apt commentary on what he was feeling by the time we reached the back edge of Dream Lake and began our ascent to Emerald Lake.

But we pushed on. When we finally reached the top, we found a beautiful, peaceful lake surrounded by mountain peaks and snow, green hues shimmering up at us from the frigid water below.

By the time we returned to our kids and Kristen, they were in the middle of their own version of snow Fruit Ninja, replicating the computer game by throwing snow in the air and cutting the chunks in half with sticks and bare hands. Then Ethan introduced us to his new chipmunk friend. "Look, Mom. He isn't leaving us and he looks like he's listening to me." And yes, the tiny rodent seemed to be hanging onto Ethan's every word before it finally got distracted and scurried off.

We continued our hike down the mountain—which went much quicker than the way up—made a stop at Bear Lake, and then waited in a long, socially distanced line to get back on the shuttle to return to our truck.

The hike into the mountains and past three beautifully unique lakes provided a peaceful respite from the outside world. We may have returned home exhausted, but it was worth it for the time together without outside distractions.

We were just going to need some time to recover.

On our second full day in Estes Park, we rested.

I spent much of the next day doing laundry, Ethan and Jeff went fishing, and Lydia painted with Kristen. It had been so long since we did peaceful, quiet things away from home, and this felt like the recharge we all needed. But I still wanted to do *one* more hike before we headed out of the mountains.

When we were finally close enough to five o'clock to be certain we wouldn't need the permit to get into the park, we packed up water and snacks, grabbed some warmer gear for the changing temperatures, and headed back up the road to Rocky Mountain National Park so we could hike to Alberta Falls.

The hike to Alberta Falls was over half a mile longer than I expected and we were approaching dinner time. Even though we made sure everyone had snacks before we left, we were still treading dangerous parenting waters. When Ethan started to exhibit hungry behavior, Kristen again saved the day with another small dose of M&Ms. We walked along a cascading river, listening to the falling water as we got deeper into the woods and higher up in elevation. Then the trail opened up to the falls, white, foamy water pouring over the large boulders, our family climbing as far as we could get to the top of the series of waterfalls.

It was everything I could have asked for on our last hike inside the national park.

The next morning, we started on the scary drive back over the mountains.

Jeff had warned me. He said when we decided to trade up to a bigger camper we were pushing it. He thought we could make it work, but it was going to be a stretch. Then he got spooked by our seriously derailed end to our summer vacation to Arches and back. We bought a much better hitch and installed it before the long haul to Big Bend for Christmas break, and it appeared to make a difference.

But then I planned for our summer vacation to Colorado. We had done smaller mountain inclines before and we were fine, kind of, although it did elevate Jeff's blood pressure a bit. When planning vacations, I had only ever looked at mileage, not the elevation the highways went through.

Our drive so far had its moments, but as we headed southwest to Black Canyon of the Gunnison, I finally began to realize just how right my husband had been about us pushing it with our F-150.

Over the course of the week we were in the Rockies, we went over one mountain pass after another, climbing up to 11,000 feet multiple times and enduring six percent grades coming down. We listened to the engine and brakes work as I prayed that we wouldn't go too fast into a vehicle in front of us or too far over into the canyon on our right. With my Colorado sister-in-law's help, we looked at alternate routes and selected the best of the bad, even though there often wasn't much of a difference.

After one particularly scary mountain pass, we somehow safely arrived at Crawford State Park, our base camp for our planned visit to Black Canyon of the Gunnison.

I had added the national park to our vacation route when I saw Instagram pictures of the canyon. When I looked at the National Parks Service website, it was on our way through Colorado. And while the drive to get to the region had been scary, I was thankful we did it as Jeff drove toward the rim of the canyon.

At first, it looked like we were in nothing but desert, surrounded by sand and sagebrush and no water in sight. Then we reached the first overlook at Tomichi Point.

Like with Cliff Palace in Mesa Verde, our first view of the national park took my breath away: black and tan walls covered in pine trees jutting out of rock and a deep canyon reaching down to the rushing Gunnison River below.

From the South Rim Visitor Center, we all followed a determined Lydia on a two-mile hike down into the canyon and then a climb back to the top. After months of sitting around and doing nothing, it seemed as if she had been lit by a spark, the previous week of exploring inspiring her to do more. And while we only did the single hike and a drive around the rim, I was so thankful I had made this one of our stops.

Our daughter's desire to explore didn't disappear as we returned to our campsite, which backed onto the reservoir lake, a small inlet immediately down the hill from where we set up camp. For three days, our kids walked up and down the hill at every opportunity, spending plenty of time together and being one with nature. They talked, Lydia sang and wrote, and Ethan threw pieces of dried mud at the shore on the opposite side of the small waterway.

After months of worrying about what was going to come next, we found an easy rhythm on the road.

Lydia and Kristen set up the tent so our daughter could fulfill her dream of sleeping outside with her aunt and having special Aunt Kristen time. The first night they had the tent up was almost awash, literally, when a serious rainstorm popped up out of nowhere, but Kristen was a seasoned Colorado camper and they made it through the night mostly dry and perfectly content.

Jeff and I took advantage of the park's biking and hiking trail to ride our bikes to the visitor center to purchase a state park magnet to add to our nearly full outdoor fridge.[2]

We survived the wind whipping across the desert for nearly every meal at the campground, forcing me to cook several meals inside.

And since we didn't feel the need to return to Black Canyon, we chose to explore another way by rafting down the river, a trip providing beautiful riverfront scenery and a little history when we took a side stop at an archaeological dig.

---

2. Ever since we bought the Roo, we have collected magnets from every place we've camped. If they are available for purchase, we buy at least one.

Then, we left behind canyons and rivers for sand dunes in the middle of the Colorado desert.

It was pitch dark as we drove into Great Sand Dunes National Park to stargaze, weaving on the road toward the parking lot next to endless hills of sand. The bright moon lit up the night, the dark outline of dunes meeting the starlit sky. Both kids ditched their shoes and ran in the sand, Lydia eventually lying down to stare up while Ethan continued running back and forth, expending days of travel energy. He didn't want to leave. He was convinced we could stay all night, especially after I mentioned people were allowed to camp in the dunes if they hiked far enough over the peaks.

We finally coaxed him away with a promise we would return the next day and I would do everything possible to find sleds so they could slide down the dunes.

The second promise proved to be a little more difficult than I originally thought.

There weren't many places outside of the park to rent sleds from, and when I finally found one, we took two of the four sleds they had left. The employees handed me wax, gave me instructions for how to use the sled, and I headed back to the campground to meet my family so we could head into the national park.

We stopped at the visitor center, purchased some items at the gift shop, collected our stamps, and picked up the Junior Ranger books and badges for our kids to finish later.

Then we headed to the dunes.

It had been too long since our kids had walked in sand. They didn't remember the struggle of the climb or the surface heat beneath their feet.

I helped Ethan lug the sled to the top of the first small dune where we waxed the back before he placed in on the sand and took off down the first hill. He worked his way through the dunes and further into the park in just that fashion, climbing to the top of one dune, sledding down, and then starting up the next one. He took to sand sledding like a champ and kept looking for better dunes to attempt.

Lydia did not do so well, discovering she preferred looking at the dunes because it was better than face-planting in the sand.

Our only major mishap of the entire day was when I returned to the truck with Lydia, who was nursing a headache and wounded pride from her last attempt at sledding, and Jeff, Kristen, and Ethan continued up the dunes.

When we returned to the base of the dunes, Lydia promptly sat down and started digging. She had no desire to continue climbing hills. I tried to call Jeff and Kristen, but no calls went through. Then I got the message, "Do you have Ethan?"

No, I didn't have our nine-year-old. I panicked.

I frantically ran to our truck, dragging Lydia behind me. Then I ran back to the sand. Then I finally saw him. "Where were you?!" I yelled as I hugged him close to me.

Through tears, my scared little boy responded, "I went to the truck like Daddy told me to."

Here I was yelling at him and he had followed my husband's directions.

It was not my best moment.

After one more night together, it was time to head home. Our family would continue the drive south. Kristen would drive north back to Denver.

Along the way, we stopped overnight at Calupin Volcano National Monument in New Mexico, and then Jeff broke his normal 300-mile-a-day limit when he suggested we break our remaining 800 miles up into two days instead of three. The vacation had been a welcome break from reality, but we were also ready to be home.

The unknowns we faced before we left for Colorado had not disappeared. We didn't know what the following school year would look like. We didn't know when vaccines would be available. We didn't know what to expect from the upcoming election. But for nearly two weeks we had proven we could safely travel and explore and leave the scary stuff behind, even if it was only temporary. At the time, it was the best we could ask for.

Chapter 35
An era ends with Campsgiving 2020

By year five, Campsgiving had become a hallowed tradition in the Styf household.

But what were we to do during a global pandemic with clear recommendations from the CDC to stay home and avoid gatherings?

Deciding to go to Colorado over the summer had seemed easy. We had such limited daily contact with people. We had essentially been hermits for three months; Jeff and I were the only ones who had contact with outsiders when we left home to run errands. When we did leave the house, we wore masks, washed our hands multiple times, and kept our interactions short.

But by November, we were already three months into the school year. The kids were in school every day and I anxiously watched my email inbox to find out if their classes were going to be the next to be quarantined. I kept my distance from my masked high school students and avoided eating lunch with my colleagues. Since the beginning of the school year, I had become increasingly reclusive, limiting my social interactions to friends I believed were being as cautious as me.

Jeff and I dove into deep conversations about the best course of action. Months earlier, before the fall surge began, we made reservations at Lake Mineral Wells State Park. There were reports that the fall was going to get bad but it seemed so far off. We invited Kristen and Jeff's parents to join us for an outdoor Texas Thanksgiving long before health officials were telling people it was the only relatively safe way for Americans to gather over the holidays.

Overall, we were lucky. None of us had gotten sick. Our jobs were stable and necessary. But like many people, it still felt like we had given up so much and our extended family was not immune to the disinformation and conspiracy theories that had been floating around for months concerning COVID-19 and the government. I had to balance my own desire for safety and fears about COVID with the need to be with family, even if everyone wasn't taking the same precautions. As we continued to make plans for Thanksgiving, my grandmother died and I missed the funeral because I didn't want to travel to Kansas and risk exposing my family after I had been exposed to a sick student. It had been the biggest blow so far of the pandemic.

Finally, after phone calls, COVID tests, intentional isolation outside of school and outdoor activities, and one anxiety-driven sobfest as Jeff tried to reassure me we were being as cautious as we could be, we packed up for our fifth annual Campsgiving trip. We were hopeful that four days of outdoor family togetherness would keep us safe while giving us the familial interaction we all craved.

Then, right before the holiday weekend, Kristen announced she was bringing Kalea with her, exciting both of our kids to know they were seeing both their favorite aunt and their favorite teenage friend. They couldn't wait to get started on the weekend.

We pulled into the state park right before dusk. Jeff nervously drove down the road below the lake rim, past a spillway, and toward the campsites.

By the time we were all set up, there was no way we were going to be exploring the park. We settled in for the night, enjoying dinner and a campfire with Jeff's family at Kristen's campsite.

But 2020 wasn't done throwing surprises our way.

As we all sat down to eat, we heard laughter and some screams in the distance. It sounded like a group of kids having fun. Then all we heard were screams.

Kalea got concerned. "Do you think those screams are something more serious?"

Nobody was sure what to think. All of the adults looked at each other. We knew which direction the screams were coming from, but not how far away they were.

"I think I should go investigate," Kalea said, but not before Kristen insisted on going with her. She wasn't letting Kalea check on screams alone.

A little while later, they returned to the campsite, giggling.

"Yeah, there's a group of college kids a few sites over, and they are pretty high. One of the girls is having a bad trip," Kristen told us.

"What does 'bad trip' mean, Mom?" Ethan asked.

I looked at Jeff.

"It means someone took drugs they shouldn't, honey. Now finish your dinner and we'll go back to the camper."

Shortly after their return, police cars and an ambulance drove into the campground, the flashing lights disrupting the still quiet of the state park, minus the incessant screaming.

I made Lydia and Ethan camp out inside our RV while the rest of us tried to figure out what was going to happen next. Then the skies opened up with a flash thunderstorm, the hail forcing Jeff and I back inside until Kristen pounded on our door. "Jeff, someone is in your truck!"

One of the other college-aged kids, also high on shrooms, had entered our truck and tried to drive off with it without keys, telling Kristen he needed to get to California when she asked what he was doing. Since he failed to drive off, he walked into another trailer down the road from us. When we went back outside to watch the conclusion of the night's events, we met the owners of the camper he entered and filled them in on what we knew. It was the most exciting start to a camping trip we had ever experienced.

Over the past year, we had chosen quiet campgrounds to escape the stress of the global pandemic. It seemed others were experimenting with different ways to escape the world seemingly falling apart around them, and we could just hope they would all be okay in the end.

By morning, the whole crew had cleared out, leaving some of their equipment in the dumpster and tent stakes all over the ground. If anything, our then nine- and eleven-year-old got a lesson in the potential dangers of hallucinogens. And we got a story worth retelling over and over again.[1]

It was a slow start to our first full day at Lake Mineral Wells because we had to move sites, which meant both cleaning our site and waiting not-so-patiently for the current occupants of our new site to pack up and leave. With the kids hanging out at Kristen's site, we moved the camper, set up at the new site, drove to the office to check in, and finally stopped at the park store to rent life jackets in case we decided to take our new kayaks out on the lake.

By the time we had moved and completed all of the "must-do" tasks, we were rapidly losing daylight. Jeff was determined to take our new inflatable kayaks—a spontaneous Amazon purchase that had spent the last month sitting on our garage floor—out on the lake. The sun was already on its afternoon descent, the temperatures were dropping below 60, and I knew the water wasn't very warm. We also had to inflate three kayaks (because Kristen had also purchased one for herself) and hope we got back to shore before it was too dark to see where we were going.

For all of the above reasons, I didn't really want to go, but it didn't matter. The rest of my family and Kristen were eager to get onto the lake and I wasn't going to be left behind. Lydia got into my kayak, Ethan got into Jeff's, and we headed out onto our very own sunset cruise. With each transition of my oar my legs got wetter and colder, but by the time we were out in the middle of the lake I forgot my misery long enough to look out at the skyline and the last rays of sun glittering on the water. The trees on the shoreline turned to black, the water around us reflecting the orange along the skyline. The water

---

1. In an additional twist, I tweeted about our experience and somehow one of the members of the group saw my tweet and reassured us that everyone in the crew ended up getting home safely.

was calm and peaceful, something I had been missing over the last several months. Despite my apprehensions, it was worth the tired arms and cold, wet clothes.

We started our Thanksgiving Day by joining many pre-dinner hikers on the Red Waterfront Trail, hiking along the gorgeous lakefront, climbing over plentiful rocks, and praying that our adventurous and fearless children wouldn't fall off of the many boulders they insisted on climbing the entire way along the trail.

When we finally returned, Jeff and I got started on Thanksgiving dinner. The kids headed over to their aunt's campsite to craft while Jeff prepared the turkey. I took care of some things around the camper before starting the rest of our Thanksgiving dinner.

By the time we were done eating, it was clear I wasn't getting the post-dinner bike ride I had longed for when I woke up in the morning. Trying out the trail would have to wait for another trip to a state park I was quickly falling in love with. Instead, I left everyone behind for a solo sunset hike along the Blue Waterfront Trail, which follows the lake from the two main camping loops. It was a break I desperately needed, and by the time I returned to the camper, nearly all of the dishes were done.

That evening, the kids crafted with Kristen and Kalea while the rest of us sat around a warm campfire that cut through the unseasonably cold temperatures. I tried to stay warm and pulled myself away from the flames when Jeff broke out the cheap telescope he had convinced me to buy on clearance from Sam's Club, hopeful we would be able to see the moon. After all of my fears and anxiety about a family Thanksgiving while a virus surged around us, I was thankful we had decided it was worth the relatively low risk.

The next morning, Jeff proved he was a good little brother when he offered to help Kristen repair her aged awning. Eventually, Jeff's parents and I were recruited to help as well.

Then the kids and I enjoyed one final adventure when they showed me the old gazebo they had found after following paths from their aunt's campsite, which was in a separate loop from ours. We had all seen the structure while kayaking out on the lake, but had no idea how to get there. While they waited for the adults to finish the work of packing up and camper repair, they had done some of their own exploring to find the "castle" structure and I was happy to oblige them with a short hike to see it for myself.

After a year of anxiety and constantly shifting norms, our Campsgiving trip was probably one of the most normal things we did in 2020. We didn't have to change our Thanksgiving traditions because our traditions took us where we were safest, especially if we kept our masks handy whenever we were going to be meeting people. And while there was still anxiety about meeting up with family, the small size of our group and the consistent outdoor activity made for as safe of a gathering as we could have hoped.

We didn't know at the time it would be our last Thanksgiving camping trip in Texas, but that is probably a good thing. It allowed us to enjoy it for what it was: the way we always wanted to celebrate the November holiday.

Chapter 36
"You said it was only two and a half miles!"

WE WERE SUPPOSED TO originally visit Palo Duro Canyon State Park at the tail end of our Arches family vacation, but when we broke down in Albuquerque, all of our plans changed. As we drove past the sign in the twilight during our marathon drive all the way home in a single night, it was a final punch in the gut from an imperfect end to a nearly perfect vacation.

We spent a single night there during our 2020 summer vacation on our way to Colorado, but it hadn't been enough for me. I realized just how much we had missed by not being able to stay in the park the first time, and a single night was not enough. So we headed west to the state park for our Christmas vacation.

I couldn't wait for our four-night stay.

The decision to camp in West Texas in December is not without risks. Winter weather in the Texas Panhandle can be unpredictable, a balmy 60 degrees one day and snow the next.[1]

Regardless, we figured the risk was worth it if we meant we could visit the park when it wasn't deathly hot and we could explore without the potential for heat exhaustion and severe dehydration.

We arrived at dusk. By the time the moon and stars rose over the canyon walls, our site was completely set up and we were ready for

---

1. Don't just assume the entire state of Texas is warm to hot all year long. If anything, the historic deep freeze we experienced two months later was a painful reminder of that fact.

dinner, the dropping temperatures and burn ban sending us inside for the night.

The next day would be for exploring.

I woke up the next morning to the sun rising over the canyon walls. I had one goal for the day: complete the Lighthouse Trail, the most popular hike in the park. The five-and-a-half-mile round trip hike takes visitors to the most famous landmark in the state park, the tall lighthouse-shaped rock towering over the second-largest canyon in the country in the park's cover photo. It is also the most dangerous hike in the park, particularly for summer visitors attempting the hike along the desert canyon floor without proper hydration and necessary rest. Thankfully, we were there during the winter. We only had to worry about temperatures that were too cold, not deathly hot.

The risk paid off. We were rewarded with perfect hiking weather: 65 degrees and sunny.

Initially, our kids tackled the trail with abandon, climbing up every set of rocks that appeared to beg for attention and doing their best to fulfill mom's Christmas wish: completing a lengthy hiking trail while on vacation. It had been a long year and I was trying to live in the moment. But that didn't mean I was willing to give up bigger goals now that the kids were older.

I had told our children the hike was two and a half miles one way, underselling the actual 2.7-mile hike. Then about one-third of the way, Ethan started complaining. "My ankle hurts."

I tried to avoid rolling my eyes, convinced he was looking for an excuse not to complete the hike. "What do you mean, your ankle hurts?"

He pointed to the back of his shoe. "It hurts right here."

After a few seconds of study, I realized a growth spurt had caused the back of his foot to rub uncomfortably against the heel of his now too small hiking shoe. I felt terrible for not believing him, but Jeff came to the rescue. He pulled out his multi-tool and cut the back of the shoe, right where it was rubbing against his ankle. We were back in business within minutes, complaints suddenly gone. It didn't hurt that I promised ice cream from the park's trading post if they completed the rest of the hike with me, *complaint-free.*

The hike took us to the base of the Lighthouse tower. Then we started the climb up the rocks to the canyon view. We paused at the top and sat on the ledge overlooking red rocks and shadowed gorges, the Lighthouse rock towering over us. When we returned to the trail, the kids booked it back, finishing the second half in half the time it took to get up to the Lighthouse. They weren't missing out on the promised ice cream and I couldn't deny them. They had earned it.

After dinner and a propane-powered fire, we said goodnight to clear skies, a bright moon, and twinkling stars. Like one month before when I sat in the kayak on Lake Mineral Wells, it was peaceful. The outside world and pandemic worries of the past year felt so far away. It had been a full day; I was ready to crash into bed.

Then we woke up to the news we had twenty-four hours before the weather would turn ugly.

The forecast for our third full day was rain and wind. We knew rain in the desert in December didn't necessarily mean we would face a lot of moisture, but the last thing we wanted was to be stuck inside during our last real day of vacation. We had done that two years before in the Davis Mountains and didn't want to do it again. Jeff also wasn't eager to start our drive home with higher-than-usual winds. Jeff and I made the call by mid-morning to leave a day early, take a different route home, and return to Houston before New Year's Eve.

That meant fitting in the rest of the things we wanted to accomplish over the next eight hours.

On our first full day in the park, Ethan had discovered a path across from our site, begging Jeff to explore to see where it led. With the help of the trail map and their bikes, they determined the trail was perfect for both hiking and mountain biking, my husband promising they could bike the trail the next day.

When I woke up for our second full day in the park, I followed the same path to the trail while our dogs stretched their legs. By the time I returned from my second dog walk, Ethan was bright-eyed and awake, ready for food and a bike ride.

He would have to wait at least two more hours before his vacationing father was ready to take him out on the trail.

They spent the late morning biking two trails as Lydia and I followed them on foot, walking and talking, me enjoying the chance to have quality alone time with my middle schooler. Teaching kept me busy, and when I wasn't working on grading or lesson planning, I was often burying myself in writing, something that had become increasingly important as I processed the pandemic. Lydia had always been our little introvert, hiding away in stories and worlds of make-believe when she was little, but increasingly following in my footsteps as she grew in her writing skills. The hike separated us from our computers and my phone and gave us time to talk—really talk—about her middle school life. She talked about her friends and her teachers, about all of the things she was learning in school and her thoughts about the future. After years of struggling to talk to my own mom, I treasured these moments, hopeful she would know I was always there for her when she needed me.

By early afternoon, we had exchanged 60 degrees for wind, overcast skies, and a high of 45. Still, Jeff decided that we were going to do the final hike I wanted to do as a family instead of leaving me to do it alone. Shortly into the canyon hike to the top of a bluff, Jeff took pity on an exhausted Lydia and offered to go back down the trail alone to pick up the truck and meet us at the top.

After warming up in the museum at the top of the trail, along the canyon rim, I thought we were done for the day. But then Jeff saw the sign for a company offering Jeep tours just outside of the park. At his insistence, I called the number from the top of the hill, the only place I had enough cell service to do so.

Thirty minutes later we found ourselves in masks, covered in blankets, and sitting across from a masked couple from Austin and their adorable little girl in the back of a topless Humvee. Over the next hour, I held on for dear life, Lydia attempted to keep herself covered in a poofy comforter, Ethan whooped like he was on a rollercoaster, and Jeff and I silently delighted at the many expressions of the little girl sitting across from us.

It was well worth the one-hour tour in the cold. We learned about the original indigenous tribes and the Comanches and Kiowas who eventually made the canyon their home. We learned about the members of the Coronado expedition who had found the canyon and searched for treasure and the ranchers who brought their cattle to the region. At the end of the drive, I took in spectacular views of the canyon we wouldn't have been able to see anywhere else, looking over a cliff edge onto the rocky bottom below.

And then we were done. And tired. And ready to put away the few items left outside so we could quickly pack up the next morning and get on the road.

When I took the dogs outside for their morning walks down the Kiowa Trail, I didn't regret our decision to leave one day early. A mist had settled over the canyon walls, permeating everything with moisture that clung to the ground, turning the red dust below my feet into cakey mud.

Once we finally left, it was a rough drive to our overnight stop in Lake Brownwood State Park, but when we checked the weather maps after our arrival we were extra relieved we had made the early departure decision—we were being followed by a snowstorm in Texas.

Jeff and I had spent the last seven years prioritizing camping as a way for our family to stay connected. Our growing kids were part of the evidence of our lives quickly changing. These longer trips helped us make memories and keep our fingers on the pulse of our kids' lives. And after a year of the world going mad, it had also helped us escape and hold onto some kind of normalcy.

Epilogue

Our family trip to Palo Duro wouldn't be our last Texas camping trip, but it would mark the end of an era. So much shifted when I lost my teaching job in mid-January.

I started this memoir six years ago, before our dream vacations out west, before COVID-19, before our lives would be turned upside down by job loss and our sudden decision six months later to uproot our family again and move back to Indiana in the summer of 2021.

As I started writing this book and began looking through pictures, remembering trips, asking questions, and trying to piece together the memories that made up the early years of our marriage and then the early years of parenthood, I began to see the constant role camping, in its different forms, played throughout the stages of our lives.

Nowhere was this truer than in the years we stopped camping altogether and the years immediately following our renewed commitment to getting out of town and back into nature.

I've never regretted each upgrade in our camping equipment. They have served as a haven and transformed our lives for the better. Camping as a whole helped me heal from the personal struggles of moving, house renovation, an emotional pregnancy, and the challenges of work and school while trying to raise a toddler and an infant, both completely dependent on their mom.

In her book *Wild*, Cheryl Strayed writes about her journey on the Pacific Coast Trail and how the weeks-long trek helped her find healing following her mother's death and a difficult divorce. At one point, ready to quit, she reflected, "I'd set out to hike the trail so that I could reflect about my life, to think about everything that had broken me and make myself whole again."[1] Shortly after this point, she realized the important lessons she had learned in such a short period of time.

> I was amazed that what I needed to survive could be carried on my back. And, most surprising of all, that I could carry it. That I could bear the unbearable. These realizations about my physical, material life couldn't help but spill over into the emotional and spiritual realm. That my complicated life could be made so simple was astounding.[2]

For us, camping is rarely "simple." It takes planning and organization and looking at calendars and finding space for all of us to be happy with our weekend plans. But once we are out there, it does simplify things. As the kids get older, it's getting harder and harder to convince them to commit to time with just their dad and me. And yes, cell phones and the television get more use these days. But our core value is always making sure we spend as much time outside and as much time together as possible.

Our camping and travel story is not over. Jeff and I hope this will continue until long after both kids have moved out of the house.

Will we always camp as part of our travels? Probably not. After all, when Jeff and I went to Hawaii to celebrate our 20th wedding anniversary, we gladly hopped on a couple of planes and slept in resorts. And someday I would like to return to Europe to show Jeff all the places I visited when I was a college student and explore more than I did before.

---

1. Strayed, Cheryl. *Wild.* Vintage Books, 2012, 84.

2. Strayed, Cheryl. *Wild.* Vintage Books, 2012, 92.

But camping is the foundation upon which my family has grown for over two decades.

It's the life I never knew I wanted. And I wouldn't want any other life than this one.

Acknowledgements

To my beta team—Jenny Owens-Cripe, Tom McCrossan, and Lucy Johnson: Thank you for all of the work you did on my book before I turned it over to Alicia to change it even more. You took my travelogue and turned it into a rough draft of a real book. Thank you for all of the hours you volunteered, for the heart you put into the project. It wouldn't be what it is now without your feedback.

To Alicia Drier: You are not just a dear friend, but a great editor. You tightened my narrative and made the words come off the page. You pushed me and stretched me and had me telling stories that were never a part of the original book. And I promise to keep working on my overuse of the word "that."

To Matt Holman: This is the second book cover you've created for me and I am so thankful I get to share your talents with the world. Thank you for so perfectly capturing our family. It is the personal touch that can only come from a 25-year friendship.

To Kate Yelland: Thank you for your proofreading work and catching the mistakes that got past Alicia and me. You added the final touch my book needed.

To Ruth and Dean Hewitt, whose legacy carries on even though your earthly story ended years before Jeff entered my life: The years my sisters and I spent exploring your Ionia farm provided a lifetime of memories. And thank you for forcing our family to explore the outdoors in my early teen years. Without those Michigan camping trips, I don't know if Mom and Dad would have ever considered camping in the Black Hills.

To John and Karen Styf: Thank you for raising your son to love camping and the outdoors and for allowing him to raid all of your camping equipment all those years ago. We continue to take good care of the fire poker that disappeared out of your garage at the same time. I don't think you're ever getting that back. We are thankful our kids have memories of Campsgiving with their grandparents during those years we didn't come "home."

To Dan and Ann Barz: Despite the incident with the tent, thank you for taking our family camping in the Black Hills. Thank you for making sure my sisters and I experienced the outdoors, even during our Detroit years. And thank you for joining us now in your retirement. I'm so glad you've decided to give camping another try, even if it is without all of your kids.

To Kristen Rollerson, who is the best big sister a woman could ask for: Your little brother may be my best friend, but you are the big sister I always needed. Thank you for taking us under your wing all those years ago when we camped up in the mountains. Thank you for coming along with us on so many adventures, for making Lydia and Ethan feel like the most special kids in the world, and for being the travel companion we have often needed. My camping story is not complete without you in it.

To Lydia and Ethan: Our family's story is just beginning, but thank you for being along for the ride. Thank you for hikes when your little legs were tired. Thank you for all the times you tried to make our anniversary special when we were traveling as a family. And thank you for still wanting to hang out with us in the national parks, even though you are now teenagers. I hope and pray these memories will help you form new experiences with families of your own someday. I love you so much.

To Jeff: None of this would be possible without you. Thank you for forcing me out of my comfort zone. Thank you for driving, even in terrible conditions. Thank you for pretending to be patient even when I'm being less than helpful while we are parking the camper. And thank you for dreaming big with me. I love you.

Works Referenced

Barz, Marilyn. *Six and a Bonus*. Marilyn Barz, 2019.

"Dinosaur Valley State Park." *Dinosaur Valley State Park Nature - Texas Parks & Wildlife Department*, 10 May 2024, https://tpwd.texas.gov/state-parks/dinosaur-valley/nature. Accessed 11 June 2024.

"Exploring Off-the-Beaten-Path Yucca House National Monument." 2019. Family Well Traveled. https://familywelltraveled.com/2019/03/09/exploring-off-the-beaten-path-yucca-house-national-monument/.

"'I'm Trapped, and Trapped for Life!'." *National Parks Service*, U.S. Department of the Interior, 23 May 2018, www.nps.gov/maca/learn/historyculture/trapped.htm.

"Mammoth Cave National Park (U.S. National Park Service)." *National Parks Service*, U.S. Department of the Interior, 22 May 2018, www.nps.gov/maca/index.htm.

"Mesa Verde National Park (U.S." n.d. National Park Service. Accessed June 27, 2024. https://www.nps.gov/meve/index.htm.

Strayed, Cheryl. *Wild: From Lost to Found on the Pacific Crest Trail*. Knopf Doubleday Publishing Group, 2013.

About the Author

Sarah Styf is a high school English teacher living just outside of Indianapolis, Indiana with her husband, two children, and two dogs. She and her husband Jeff have spent the last twenty years of their marriage exploring campgrounds around the United States. She and her family have now camped in twenty-nine of the fifty states. You can get her first book, *Embracing the Journey: Learning to Grow When Life Doesn't Work Out as Planned*, as an e-book, paperback, or audiobook, anywhere books are sold. You can also follow more of her travels by subscribing to her newsletter: www.sarahstyf.substack.com.